Mission

America

Scott Mann

MISSION AMERICA

WHAT YOU NEED TO COME HOME...
IS ALREADY INSIDE YOU.

This book is dedicated to Sergeant Eric Landon.

Warrior. Husband. Father.

He was a casualty of combat.

Long after the guns of war had fallen silent,

Eric's battle still raged on.

He took his own life on July 30th, 2015.

May his memory always remind us of our duty as Americans to bring our warriors home to a life of honor and peace.

ISBN-10: 0-9981759-0-0

ISBN-13: 978-0-9981759-0-4

Published by

The Heroes Journey
10312 Bloomingdale Ave, Ste 108-193
Riverview, FL 33578
Website: www.theheroesjourney.org

For bulk purchases and speaking engagements, contact:

The Heroes Journey
10127 Albyar Ave
Riverview FL 33578
910-584-1474
contact@theheroesjourney.org

Because of the dynamic nature of the Internet, web addresses or links contained in this book may have changed since publication and may no longer be valid.

The author of this book does not dispense medical, legal, or psychological advice, nor does he suggest any technique as a form of treatment for medical, physical, or emotional problems. Always consult the appropriate professional. Your use of the information in this book for yourself is your responsibility; you are responsible for the actions and outcomes resulting from the use of the information contained herein. The author assumes no responsibility or liability for the outcome of those actions.

Editor: Mark Tompkins

Layout/Cover/Illustrations: Todd Day

Publishing and Release Support: The Solution Machine

CONTENTS

Introduction: Why this book?

What no one told you about transition

"Getting out of the military scares the shit out of me!" I talk to warriors and their families all the time about military transition to the civilian world. This is one of the most common phrases they say to me.

We need some straight talk here.

Transition poses challenges to just about every veteran and military family member one way or the other.

Every year, over 200,000 military service members transition into American civil society. For many, it's not going well. In fact, military transition is broken.

It's a problem that nearly kicked my ass. It's a problem that is kicking the ass of many of my brother and sister warriors.

Maybe it's kicking yours? Or, maybe you're still serving, but don't like to even think about it. It doesn't have to be this way.

Fork in the road

As I see it, there are two choices:

Choice One: We can wait for someone to come and fix transition.

Choice Two: We handle this ourselves.

I'm going with Choice Two. You — me — us. No one else is coming.

Sure, there are lots of organizations trying to help with military transition. Whether it's a cattle drive retreat out west or military family immersions in luxurious beach spas, or something in between, there are so many people trying to help. It's a 'sea of good will' out there as over 40,000 nonprofit organizations clamor to help veterans transition from the military.

In fact, there are so many veteran advocacy organizations out there that it's downright paralyzing. Where the hell do you even start?

That's the real reason I got involved. As I went through my own transition, it seemed like all these well-intentioned folks in the Department of Defense, Veterans Administration, and the numerous nonprofits were focusing on good things but they didn't quite scratch the itch of what I was going through.

There was something else going on inside me that needed to be addressed. Dozens more of my peers told me the same thing as time went on.

That's why I wrote this book.

EVERYTHING OLD IS NEW AGAIN

Military transition isn't new. Warriors have faced the timeless challenge of returning to civil society since Odysseus had his unlucky ass blown unmercifully across the seven seas.

But how we return home is really tricky these days. If we aren't careful, we end up becoming something we think society wants us to become instead of who we are...warriors.

In this book, I'll show how that path can lead to a range of bad things, including general unhappiness. And for me, I'm just not in the mood to be generally unhappy after serving my time in the military. I'm ready to live a bigger, fuller life. If that resonates with you, keep reading.

Answering the question of who we are as warriors, and how to live the life we were meant to live after the guns go silent by using what we already have inside of us, is the aim of this book.

To do that, I am going to talk really straight about what transition means:

to you, the veteran.

to your loved ones and family.

to the American civilian who must help us come home.

to the employer and lender trying to bring veterans into the private sector.

The stuff we'll talk about here you won't find in your traditional transition program. Your chain of command probably won't talk to you about it. But it's the stuff that every single warrior should be thinking about, and as early as possible.

WHAT THIS BOOK IS ABOUT

The concept for this book is simple:

If you are a warrior (past or present) or military family member: Just about everything you need for transition is already inside you. I will help you locate it.

If you are a civilian looking to help warriors with transition, you have a lot to offer and we need you to help at a community level. I will help you figure out how.

YOUR MISSION AMERICA ROUTE MAP

I will explore how we reconnect the warrior with the civilian for a life of prosperity and a better America. To do that, I've divided this book into three parts. It's a user guide, so feel free to jump to any part in the book that interests you or read it in its entirety. It's completely up to you.

For the digital version, there are multiple hyperlinks to help you move effortlessly within the book as well as access resources outside of the book. Let's look at how I've organized our journey together.

Part I is the "mindset for transition." In this section, we'll look at the internal challenges, which I call 'snakes in the head,' that military transition will throw your way. We'll also look at the various mindset and resilience components that are critical to dealing with all the 'snakes' that might slither your way.

Part II is focused on the "skill set for transition." There are three primary skills I believe are essential for transition that you already have inside you that should be redirected: storytelling, collaboration to build out your transition 'team room,' and intelligence and operational preparation of your new transition environment.

(Note: Civilians, never fear...even if you don't know what these Part II terms mean, dive in and learn more about how our world works.)

In Part III, civilians will find particularly helpful information for locating their role in this critical mission — that of reconnecting warriors to our civil society. The level of support from the American people is enormous, but we still have a long way to go to fully leverage the full power of citizen support toward our transition.

WHO THIS BOOK IS FOR

"When I left Fort Stewart, Georgia I was so happy to be free," admits Army veteran Jon Burnson.
"But this transition is anything but easy."

Mission America is for any veteran — past or present — who is struggling with any aspect of transition to civil society.

You don't have to be a combat veteran. There are a lot of references in this book to recent military combat service, but many warriors who never went to war undergo transition challenges. Some of these go on for decades. This book is for every warrior who has made the journey home or who will have to do it one day.

"Even though Desert Storm had ended by the time I had completed my training and other conflicts didn't occur until years after I was honorably discharged," says former Marine Joshua Olmsted, "I still had a tough time transitioning back to civilian life. To be honest, I still struggle from time to time out here in civilian life. I miss the Corps and the brotherhood that I had while I was enlisted. Nothing compares to that. I miss it badly."

I also wrote this book for those of you who have been out for a while but still haven't quite found your fit. I've spoken with so many Vietnam veterans, for example, who are still struggling to return home.

Mission America is also for citizens who never served in the military but care deeply about bringing our veterans home with honor.

Everyone reading this book will have unique reasons for doing so. But what binds us is a desire for a better America.

Reconnecting warriors and civilians is a great place to start!

WHAT IT AIN'T!

Mission America won't fix your transition problems.

Only you can do that.

Please don't look outside yourself for the most critical answers to your new life. There are no shortcuts in here. Transition, no matter what you plan to do for a living, requires work.

There is no "easy button."

Transition is a long-term process. Just as it took a while to build your military skill set and credibility, transition to civilian endeavors is no different.

Expectation management is important for you and your loved ones when it comes to returning home.

You never really *arrive*, do you?

The old saying "It's not the destination, but the journey that counts" has never been more accurate.

Viewing your transition as a lifelong mission — MISSION AMERICA — is one of the best things you can do for you and your loved ones.

And that's what this book is all about!

MY PROMISE TO YOU

When you finish this book, you'll know really helpful transition stuff — things that will stretch your comfort zone — that no one else is going to talk to you about in job fairs and transition workshops.

I'm going right for your solar plexus and your heart. This is the only way to get at the good, the bad, and the ugly of transition.

I am going to help you think about the things keeping you up at night. You know, the internal stuff, that often seems unique to you as a warrior — things that visit you at night, when your eyes are wide open and the rest of the world sleeps. I know, because I have seen them too.

Although we're honest about transition, this is not a gloom-and-doom prognosis.

In fact, the opportunities for new dreams and personal freedom have never been greater.

If you'll open your mind, take these points to heart, and apply them in earnest, you will vastly decrease your learning curve over these transition challenges and open new doors you never thought possible.

Anyone who guarantees your dreams to come true is a snake oil salesman. Beware of that. But the chance to **pursue** your dreams with the optimum odds for success…that, fellow Spartans, is EXACTLY what you deserve.

I believe history will judge us in this critical endeavor, so let's get this right.

PART I
MINDSET FOR TRANSITION

1

RONIN...

But what about us? What about the soldier or
Marine who steps off the plane from overseas and
finds himself in the scariest places he's seen in
years?

Home.
— Steven Pressfield, *The Warrior Ethos*

A SOLDIER THROUGH AND THROUGH

I am a soldier.

I always have been. Since I was 14 years old.
Well, kind of...

That's when I decided to become a Green
Beret. I was a scrawny kid growing up in a little
Arkansas logging town. I faced enough personal
failure and social isolation that I might as well have
been a Spartan boy enrolled in the *agoge*.

Weighing 105 lbs., soaking wet, the only thing
remarkable about me was how physically
unremarkable I was. Nothing about my stature
indicated that I would ever become a warrior.

Except maybe my heart.

The day I became a warrior is still very clear in

my mind. I saw a real, honest-to-goodness Green Beret in our Mount Ida, Arkansas soda shop.

That did it. He even spoke to me.

From that point on, I knew what I wanted.

It would be another 15 years before my dream of Special Forces became a reality.

But I never wavered — I never faltered in my pursuit of that dream. And on the day I earned my Green Beret in October 1996, I spent the rest of my adult life stomping around rough places in the world — living the dream of that 14-year-old kid.

I fought wars. I trained armies. I lived the Spartan life that many men fantasize about. Got pretty damn good at it, too.

But what happens when that dream ends?

What happens when everything that defined you comes to an an end? When you become...a Ronin. A samurai without a master.

Shit gets real. That's what happens.

That new reality led me to write this book. Well, that and the snakes.

2

"SSSSSSSSS"

HANGING UP THE BOOTS

Finally! After almost 23 years in the Army, it was time to retire. I was ready, I had everything planned out.

Not more than three days after hanging up my desert boots, and putting on my Tampa Bay flip-flops, they started to squirm.

Snakes. Snakes in my head.

I first heard that eerie phrase describing post-service challenges from my longtime mentor and Vietnam-era Green Beret, Dave "Doc" Phillips.

He patiently explained to me, shortly before I retired, that although everything seemed on track in my life, "the snakes would likely start to slither" at some point. The snakes he referred to were all the stressors of transition, combat, and everything else that would come home to roost once the uniform was off.

Dave assured me that when they did, he'd be there when I needed him.

Thanks, Doc. You were right on.

Of course, I quickly dismissed his words after

hearing them. It didn't seem possible that anything could go wrong with my well-oiled plan. How could it?

Not only was I finally done with Uncle Sam, but I had a helluva course plotted out. This plan included a nice real estate portfolio of passive income that, combined with my Army retirement pay, left me financially free. (In other words, my passive income from my real estate checks was greater than my monthly expenses.)

My wife and I were still in love and very much enjoyed our time together. My three boys Cody, Cooper, and Brayden were still young and living at home. We bought a home on the Alafia River in Tampa. It was perfectly 'off the grid.'

I was finally going to write that book on my lessons learned from Afghanistan. Despite my changing from fatigues to civilian clothes, military units still wanted me to continue training their units.

Everything was set. No — everything was PERFECT!

REALITY BITES

Then it happened. Despite all these positive factors in my life, some pretty big anacondas started slithering slowly around in my head. Let me give you a few examples of what I mean by this:

I totally underestimated the length of time I'd been away from home during my career. Turns out, my family had learned to get by pretty well without me.

Who knew?

They actually had to learn to deal with me being around more. That wasn't very much fun to discover.

Now that I was home — a lot more — family comfort zones were stretched on all sides. I felt like a foreigner in my own house. Oh well, at least I had my new, uh, career.

It was nothing like the career of wearing that Army uniform. Sometimes, I missed Special Forces so badly I could taste it. The brotherhood I had known since I was a young man was not as easy to leave as I'd thought.

Maybe it was because I didn't see much of a brotherhood on the outside at all. It seemed like the most cutthroat and selfish world I'd ever seen. No one had my back. Every man for himself. How the hell was I ever going to fit in here?

And what was I supposed to do, anyway? Who was I fooling? When I wore that uniform I knew exactly who I was, and where I stood…even on the really crappy days. My sense of self and sense of purpose were totally clear.

Not anymore.

It was all hazy now. Sometimes, I felt like I was losing my mind as my moods went up and down like a roller coaster. My wonderful little boys who had endured so much separation and anxiety for so long walked on eggshells around me. They quietly asked each other, and their Mom, "What in the world is wrong with Dad?"

Unfortunately, my wife didn't know what to tell them. She was just as dumbfounded by all of this as they were.

She would ask me desperately through screamed whispers in our bedroom: "What is the matter with you?! We have waited for years to have time together and now, everything is so stressful and strained? Why can't you be happy?! What the hell is going on?!"

Snakes, baby. That's what.

3

MORE SNAKES

LIFE HAPPENS...

"Hey sir, they just passed me over for major."

Rob's words pierced the air as I listened to his voice crack over the phone. Although he was usually as cool as a cucumber, I could hear his pain through the phone.

"I feel like someone just kicked me in the nuts," he said quietly.

I listened in disbelief. I had been one of Rob's mentors since 2010. This prior service Green Beret captain was one of the strongest detachment commanders I ever worked with.

Now, instead of excitedly planning for his next assignment to his mid-career officer training course, like his peers, he was about to become a civilian within a year. His life was flipped upside down.

The snakes of military transition come in all shapes and sizes. For me it was trying to fit in to civilian life after 20+ years of military service. For Rob, and many of you, it was running 90 mph on military missions only to find out you're being turned out way before you planned.

RUNNING HARD

"Scotty, there are two phases of your life now," Ed Reeder, my former commander, said to me not long after those towers fell on September 11th, 2001. "You are either at war, or getting ready to go back. So get used to it."

The hard-nosed officer couldn't have been more accurate. Even when we weren't deployed, most of us were training our asses off and getting ready to go again. It wasn't just Green Berets. This was true of almost every military unit, including the National Guard and Reserve forces.

The fight we are in today isn't going away anytime soon. The end of the Global War on Terror is just another beginning of more campaigns against shadowy threats like ISIS — as well as new threats from our age-old enemies, like China and Russia.

We maintained this operational tempo with a very small force. The wartime demands of Iraq and Afghanistan along with other deployments put unprecedented demands on our force.

While the military operational and deployment tempo continues, our force is shrinking. Thanks to congressional budget constraints, military services are thinning their ranks by tens of thousands.

Many of our warriors are training so hard and deploying so much, they have almost no time to think about transition from the military. Most of them still have dust on their boots and gunpowder residue on their hands when they show up for their 10 days of mandatory transition training.

Whether military transition is planned or unexpected, the thought of civilian life causes snakes to squirm in warrior noggins all over America. Why wouldn't it?

Our economy still struggles. Unemployment rates are high. Despite well-intended government and corporate hiring programs, veteran unemployment rates are still way too high.

What about contractor jobs? Those are diminishing in tandem with the military drawdown.

"I'd rather go back to Afghanistan four more times in a row than go through transition." This was what a Special Forces master sergeant whom I'll call "Gary" said to me as he was starting his transition process.

I had known Gary for years. He had seen more combat, lost more friends, and endured more heartache than almost any warrior I knew. No one was more anxious for stillness of the guns than Gary.

Yet he would rather go back to that hellish combat four more times than to ever go through transition again. How could this be?

Some of us carry snakes from the toll of service. We've given a lot — maybe more than we realize.

Some of us are pretty scuffed up as well. Indeed, tens of thousands of us have endured grievous wounds and even more bear internal wounds and trauma that we are only now starting to see.

As a veteran, whether you saw combat or not, you likely sacrificed massive amounts of time away from home that you will never get back. Many of our families are strained, if not broken. For some of us, we've seen many friends die — and their memory still haunts us.

But the most common snake of all? Well, that

seems to be fear of leaving the world we know and understand — the U.S. military.

THE UNSPOKEN FEAR

Transition represents uncertainty of the highest order. Civilian life is a world we know nothing about.

I think the fear of transition starts the day we come in the military.

That's because transition is about losing our security blanket — which is all of the things Uncle Sam took care of, so that we could focus on executing missions.

Although our missions were rough, there were plenty of benefits:

We always knew where our pay was coming from. We knew our families would be cared for. Family healthcare was as easy as your spouse making a quick call to the base clinic for an appointment. (In 1999 at Fort Bragg, North Carolina, the birth of my first child cost my wife and me a whopping 12 dollars at the base hospital.)

For most of us, we could actually sit down with our supervisor or a career manager and map out our professional goals five years out and be fairly sure we could follow that path. Now, all that has changed.

And lastly, let's not forget that we have changed as warriors. We've literally lived the hero's journey...never to return home the same man or woman we were when we said goodbye.

Yeah, we've all got snakes, but who doesn't? As warriors we've faced challenges our whole life.

Despite these challenges, the opportunities in front of you have never been greater. As you'll

see, if you keep reading this book, most of the skills needed to transition from the military and into a life of prosperity and happiness are already inside of you. It's all in how you choose to think about it.

But first...we need a new story.

4

THE TRUTH...ABOUT SNAKES

TAMPA, FLORIDA, 2011

"I just feel so sorry for you guys. What can we do to help you?" This lady, pity on her face, was a total stranger who came up to me in a restaurant a few years ago after seeing me in my uniform. She meant well as she patted me on the arm. I smiled sheepishly and didn't really know what to say.

I remember thinking that if this is how warriors are viewed today, we're going to have a big problem down the road.

Fast-forward to today, and my concerns have come true. Have you listened to the overall narratives about veterans across America? I don't like any of them.

To my brother and sister warriors, it starts with us. No one will craft the accurate narrative that serves our nation and our veterans unless we start it.

No one will tell the compelling stories of what transition really looks like at the community level unless we start the process.

We have to think strategically, accept the

need to punch above our weight, and take the microphone back from some well-intended but misguided spokespeople.

THE WRONG STORIES...

Let's start with what I call the *"damaged goods"* narrative. A lot of well-meaning nonprofit organizations have helped create this one.

Passionate videos and pleas from teary-eyed celebrities and entertainers convey an image of a warrior community that tugs on the heartstrings. But it's not representative of our veteran community.

It makes us look, well…broken.

Sure, there are some gravely wounded veterans (inside and out) who are broken — they will need our nation's help and care for the rest of their lives. The response by Americans and nonprofit groups to care for these heroes is wonderful. But that's just a single drop of water in a sea of powerful stories from our American veteran community.

Then there is the *"We don't understand you"* narrative. This is the one that many civilians feel deep down, but don't know how to talk about. So let's break it down right here.

"Scott, how can you convince employers that hiring a veteran isn't risky? How do you overcome the fear of hiring people like the disturbed young man who killed Navy SEAL Chris Kyle in the blockbuster movie *American Sniper*?" This question came to me from a local entrepreneur who was interested in a TEDx Talk I was preparing on veteran transition.

This narrative goes even further by portraying veterans not only as "the island of misfit toys," but as potentially unstable due to combat exposure, and a risk to businesses and society. Just not true.

Admittedly, many veterans have seen a lot of combat. Some have been fighting the longest war in our nation's history. Combat is a corrosive environment and it leaves its imprint on even the toughest warrior.

The majority of these folks aren't damaged goods. They are some of the most reliable men and women on the planet!

I'll admit, as they come home, there are some challenges to deal with. I had mine — still do.

But who doesn't? These are not insurmountable obstacles that require a life of being cared for. They are simply microrealities that should be dealt with so we can get these badass high performers back into the game to help lead our nation and our communities.

Finally, there is the *"Thanks for your service, here's a job"* narrative. This one, also well-intended, is off the mark when it comes to our veterans finding their path to happiness and prosperity. Equally important, it undervalues the real contribution potential of our veterans.

While I'm impressed by the vast number of jobs and hiring programs that our government and big companies are attempting to put out there, it's a flawed approach.

Transition from the military is more than just finding a job — even a high-paying job. Not all of today's warriors are cut out to just shed the uniform and become a park ranger (unless of course, your goal is to become a park ranger).

The point is, rather than create these big job programs and call it a day, we've got to go deeper. An all-volunteer force with an enormous and recurring deployment tempo adds more strain than just getting a job. These multiple challenges are best addressed by connecting warriors and civilians at a community level. That informal partnership helps our veterans and their families find the path to best fit into civil society for the greater good and their own personal dreams.

Just taking a job right out of the gate of transition might answer short-term needs, but as we'll see in this book, it doesn't get you where you need to go.

THE RIGHT STORY...

The American military always ranks higher than just about any other group or institution when it comes to trust by Americans.

These are men and women with an honor-based warrior ethos that is unparalleled in today's civilian world. Trust me, these are leaders that many struggling American communities sorely need to lead them.

We may be a little scuffed up, but our scars and bruises are some of our greatest assets. Warriors are not a group of people who need to be 'cared for,' nor do we want to be. We are the ones who want to 'care for' America, abroad — and at home.

Our warriors and families protect our society and everything it stands for. Having these instinctive protectors among us makes us safer, not more at risk.

The resilience of returning American warriors, and their families, to help America overcome complex problems at home is a great story. A similar one resonated across the country after World War II as hundreds of thousands of fighting men and women led the country to new heights of prosperity. Why can't that be the new narrative today?

It's time to change all of these narratives to reflect the local reality of our warriors and the communities where you will live. This means <u>civilians</u> and <u>veterans</u> working together to tell a better story.

Time to take the mic!

5

YOUR MISSION, SHOULD YOU CHOOSE TO ACCEPT IT...

HELP WANTED...

"Hey, if you know anyone who is hiring...let me know, OK?" If I had a dime for every time someone leaving the military asked me this question, I'd be the richest Army dude in retirement.

If you served, you've probably heard this too — or maybe you have posted your own "I'm getting out, anyone wanna hire me?" post on LinkedIn.

When getting out of the service, most of us worry first and foremost about finding work. And why shouldn't we?

We have to put food on the table, provide for our family, start a new life. This is what every other veteran does when she goes back to *the world*, right? Wrong.

Transition is more than just getting a job. And if you think finding work, post-service, is all there is, you'd better get ready to meet some snakes in the head.

Successful transition involves every aspect of who you are, what you stand for, and where you are going.

I've said that many transition attributes are already inside of you: Let's reflect on your life in the military for a minute.

Did you succeed as a warrior by singularly graduating from basic training or learning your initial entry technical skill? Of course not.

Sure, that was part of it, but there was much more to the equation. There was much more to you.

A DEEPER LOOK

Military service members, by nature, are pros. There is no patience in our line of work for amateurs.

As a warrior, you had a professional mindset, complete with an internal goal that drove you, didn't you? To meet it, you conditioned your mind, body, and spirit to work in unison. Even those of you who came in without a clue, likely set your sights on some kind of objective pretty early in the service. It's how we're conditioned and trained.

To do this, you had to get to know yourself, warts and all.

You knew the gaping holes that stood between you and your military ambitions, and the risks those gaps posed to reaching your goals.

To reach them, you did whatever it took, even if you had to pursue additional training, study on your own, and build your intelligence and capacity in new fields. You would even spend your own money on better gear than the crap the government gave you, to get a competitive edge, wouldn't you? Why the hell do you think there is a U.S. Cavalry, Ranger

Joes, or other high-end tactical gear store just outside the gate of every military post in America?

Investing in your tradecraft is just what pros do.

For all the work you did on your own, there were still a few gaps that remained between you and your goal, right? And for those, you probably reached out to your teammates and other military subject matter experts to help fill them.

Well, transition is no different.

USING WHAT YOU ALREADY HAVE

Transition requires a dedicated, holistic approach that goes way beyond just getting a job. In fact, many of the same techniques you used in the military to meet your goals will also apply in transition.

"You want to know how I did it?" The highly successful CEO and former Special Ops sergeant major named Bruce looked straight at me. He was explaining to a group of assembled veterans and entrepreneurs how he had gone from military service to a multimillion-dollar company. **"I used what I already knew how to do. You know, I treated transition like it was another mission."**

There it is! Every warrior I've talked to, who has kicked transition smooth in the ass, says about the same thing:

The same mindset and skill set we need to live a life of prosperity and happiness in the civilian world are already inside us.

In Phil Randazzo's book *Mission Next*, an employer named Greg explains, "The reason I like hiring veterans is because they understand commitment. They are one of the few people who can put on a résumé: *'willing to take a bullet for my former employer.'"*

"The returning warrior may not realize it," says best-selling author and former Marine Steven Pressfield, "but he has already acquired an MBA in enduring adversity, and a Ph.D in resourcefulness, tenacity, and the capacity for hard work."

"Talk to us in a language we understand." This is one of the number one themes I hear from NCOs and officers when they describe their frustrations and pain points with current transition programs. Transition is better understood when we look through lens of what we already know — a mission. Mission America.

6

BOOTS ON A WIRE

FORT BENNING, GEORGIA, 1995

The old infantry first sergeant was drunk as hell. But you could still see the pain in his eyes as he nursed his beer and lamented his upcoming retirement.

He taught me a lot as a young officer, and just weeks from retirement, he was giving me his last lesson. "El Tee (LT) — don't you ever forget this. The Army will replace you quicker than they'll replace those fucking boots on your feet."

Some things never change.

Despite the warnings from that old top sergeant, I waited too long to believe that little nugget of information. I really thought my departure was going to be a real blow to the U.S. Army and the Special Operations community. Did they have any idea how badly they'd miss me? How would they get by?

The old top sergeant was right: The day after you leave the service and sling your old boots up on the nearest telephone wires, the U.S. military will replace you quicker than they do those boots.

Sure, many of the men and women whom you served with will miss you. They shake their heads sadly and probably speak of you fondly. But they will go on — and do just fine.

Nothing will fail without you. Nothing will fall through the proverbial cracks that can't be repaired quickly. Your spot in the unit and your role in what you thought was that irreplaceable warrior niche will be filled before the keg is empty at your retirement party. That's just how it goes.

Accepting this reality sooner rather than later is one snake you can easily dispatch before you even take off your uniform.

7

"PERMISSION TO DO MY THING, SIR?"

TAMPA, FLORIDA, 2015

I was about to throw up. "What am I doing?! What will my brothers think of me?"

It was time to hit SEND, and launch the final version of my book, *Game Changers*, to the publisher. Instead, I sat paralyzed in front of my keyboard as my mind agonized over more daunting questions: "What if this book makes my former bosses mad? What if they don't like it?"

At this point I did what I'd done at every tough crossroads in life. I called my dad, Rex. Just as he'd done with every tough challenge in my life, my dad had helped me with every step of the book. Surely he'd understand the dilemma facing me and tell me it was cool to just not publish the book right now. I should've known better.

As he picked up the phone, I frantically asked, "Dad, who the hell am I to be writing something like this?" In his country drawl that was always so soothing to me in these situations, he said, "Scotty, who are you not to? Don't cheat us out of this book."

"Hell with it," I said out loud. "SEND."

That was the first time after leaving the military that I came face to face with this vulnerability, of seeking unnecessary permission for my life in transition.

CRAWLING OUT OF THE BUCKET

In the military we live such a rigid lifestyle. Even in Special Operations, everything is taken care of, from our monthly paycheck to where we're moving next. This rigidity and chain of command serves a purpose and we become quite entrenched in the process.

"The Marine Corps is like an earning thing. It's an honor culture," said former Marine William Treseder in an interview with American Dream U. "You have to really earn where you are. It gave me a set of objective criteria across physical, mental, and moral standards."

Honor and status as a warrior are huge, aren't they? That said, we are also prone to look to our military peers, whom we immensely respect, for permission to get outside our comfort zones. That's OK for thinking through a new concept or strategy in the service, but not in real life. It holds you back, big time!

Have you ever watched crabs in a bucket? What happens when one makes it almost to the top of the bucket?

The other crabs pull her back down into the bucket.

But here's the thing, it's not that our former teammates actually pull us down. We just think they might. Truth is, most of our former commanders and military peers are, as Steve Pressfield says, "so caught up in their own shit that they could care less about what we do."

And as for the ones who *do* feel like they should grant us permission? And yeah, there are a few 'toolbags' who fit this category, who are so miserable and full of self-loathing, they aren't worth the time it takes to deal with them. They are going to be miserable no matter what. That's why they troll the Internet looking for ways to blast others so they can point to who they used to be, instead of who they are becoming.

Those that matter in the real scheme of things will be happy for you, and the minority of folks who really are crabs...well, they're just fucking crabs. What do they have to do with your life and your dreams?

"I hire lots of military veterans in my company," an Internet marketer named Dave told me. "They are incredible, and their work ethic far surpasses their peers who haven't served."

"Here is my only concern," Dave told me candidly. Many of the veterans he hires seem to be holding back a little bit. It's as if they're waiting to be told it's OK to run. "I get enough of that from civilians. I wanna see more of the '*I got this shit*' mindset that characterizes the American warrior," he concluded. I have talked to a ton of CEOs and they feel the same way.

If we're not careful, this mindset can infiltrate our transition like a stealthy sniper, and our misapplied quiet professionalism can kill our dreams before they ever take root.

The tendency is to hold back, to be measured, and it will likely happen to you. But

when it comes to transition, you can't wait for permission to pursue your dreams — ever.

For me it was a book; for you, it is something different. **You may find yourself holding back and wondering if it's OK to do what you're doing or what others will think about your actions. Screw that.**

You've waited long enough and put your life on hold so that others can chase their dreams. You don't need permission, and if you do…I'm giving it to you right here, right now.

Even with permission, there's TNT inside you that has fueled your warrior actions for years. Let's go to the next chapter and see how to put that to work.

8

DYNAMITE AND JUMPSUITS

"I'm going to prison." This dude was addressing hundreds, but he was speaking right to me.

His name was Bo Eason, former NFL football player, playwright, and leadership coach. Even though he shared the gut-wrenching story of blowing out his knee and his departure from the NFL, he was telling my story — and the story of every other warrior I'd ever met.

He described being carried off the field and the surreal feeling he had as he reflected on the 20-year plan he'd followed since he was nine years old: to become the best safety in the NFL.

Now, on a stretcher, as he made his way to the locker room for the last time, reality struck him. Every skill he had developed for as long as he could remember involved knocking the shit out of people. Voted "the dirtiest player in the NFL," this brutal tradecraft was now going to land him in prison if he didn't find a new path.

What the hell was he going to do?

Bo's life was running his head into people's chests. He had to find a way to turn that TNT inside him into something positive.

REDIRECTING THE DYNAMITE

Like many of you reading this, I had run a similar path to Bo — not in the NFL, but in the game of life and death. To make it into Special Forces, I had run my own 20-year plan. I had wanted to be a Green Beret since I was 14 years old. Every memory I had involved training to become a Green Beret.

Now, as I prepared to leave the corrosive arena of combat that had chewed so many of us up, I had to avoid the orange jumpsuit as well.

I did it by redirecting that internal dynamite into new forms of expression that still serve something bigger than me. For me, this redirection includes writing, storytelling, and helping other veterans. These are my passions today.

How about you? How will you redirect your TNT? Let's start figuring it out.

9

OF PURPOSE AND PASSION...

PROVO, UTAH, 2016

"I had no purpose anymore." Former Marine officer and jet pilot Chad Tucker was telling me this not long after he medically retired from the service. "I was in some dark places, man."

Chad isn't the only one. This loss of purpose can lead to another frustrated statement — usually with a tinge of panic — from transitioning warriors: "I have no idea what I am passionate about."

This reality can strike fear in the heart of the biggest, baddest warrior. Here's why.

Despite our rough-and-tumble image, and the downtrodden images portrayed by some well-meaning nonprofit groups, most veterans I've worked with (thousands, actually) are happy people.

Whether it's on a six-month "Navy Float" to the Mediterranean Sea like Chad did, conducting patrols from fire bases hundreds of miles from known civilization, or operating Air Force missions out of bare base airfields, you will usually find warriors grinning from ear to ear whenever they are doing their mission. Why? Purpose.

Warriors usually have a strong sense of purpose to serve something bigger than themselves.

That purpose naturally aligns with life in the military, doesn't it? Answering that higher calling becomes as natural as lacing those boots up every morning.

But too often, we project the military as our singular purpose, and not the vehicle to achieve it.

The military gives us an amazing platform to fulfill our sense of purpose, which usually feels pretty damn good. Alignment of mind, body, and spirit usually does.

But what if instead of looking at the military as answering the big "Why" in our life, we shifted it a bit. What if we looked deeper inside ourselves for our "Why" and viewed the military as our "What" and "How" of achieving that "Why."

This simple shift in thinking is decisive.

FINDING YOUR WHY

I've seen too many warriors get chewed up not paying attention to this one. Getting this distinction straight is the most important thing we can do before stepping into transition.

"It takes time for a warrior to make his or her combat experience meaningful," cautions former Marine officer David J. Danello. Dave was a seasoned combat leader in the Iraq War, and in his book *The Return*, he takes on some of the toughest questions warriors must face as they come home from war.

"What is your calling, your real one, not your job title or military occupational specialty?" Danello asks. "What offers you excitement, enthusiasm, and purpose?"

Remember, passions (even those we defined as warriors) come and go.

Purpose is forever.

10

THE MYTH OF UNPAID DUES

ORLANDO, FLORIDA, 2014

Miserable.

The guy in front of me was miserable.

He tried to sound upbeat. But this recently retired Army colonel was really unhappy.

We were discussing his new military contracting job. He was assuring me — unsolicited, mind you — that, although he didn't like his job, it was the best possible option for him.

"It's a pretty good job. It feeds my family. I mean, I'm not crazy about what I am doing now, but after doing what I loved for 28 years in the military, I guess it's time for me to grow up and pay my dues."

Bullshit. It doesn't have to be this way. And it's dangerous to you and your loved ones if it is.

11

RESETTING YOUR TRANSITION COMPASS

"People don't buy what you do, they buy WHY you
do it."
— Simon Sinek, *Start with Why*

FORT BENNING, GEORGIA, 1992

"Gentlemen, the American warrior will achieve the
most difficult mission in the world — no matter
how rough the circumstances — as long as he
knows the answer to one simple question…WHY!"

I will never forget this piece of advice I
received from Sergeant First Class Price. He was
teaching a gaggle of bald-headed Ranger students
how to develop Commander's Intent for a 5
Paragraph Operations Order.

Over a decade later, I witnessed unprecedented
heroism every single day by dozens of our nation's

finest warriors. They achieved magnificent outcomes in combat with little more than a task and purpose given to them.

In military mission planning, we always lead off with the Commander's Intent. This is an essential component of every mission. When time is short, we often leave out parts of mission planning — but Commander's Intent, which focuses on **purpose,** is never left out.

Explaining to your troops WHY they are conducting a mission ensures that they will find a way to accomplish it no matter how ambiguous and chaotic the battlefield becomes.

If every senior leader is killed off, the lowest-ranking American warrior will persevere and overcome all, as long as he knows WHY he is doing it. Let's transfer this effective military planning into transition thinking, except with one small shift:

COMMANDER'S INTENT HAS CHANGED!

YOU are the Commander (you have to give yourself permission for this) and your intent is the key to what happens next in your transition journey. This requires you to be intentional and focused on connecting to your higher purpose.

With this mindset, you can figure anything out about transition and beyond, as long as you know your purpose. Everything else will fall into place.

My leadership coach Jerry Lujan calls it discovering your "why." I call it true north. My dad calls it "leaving tracks." They all mean the same thing…the inner compass that guides us toward our reason for being on this earth.

Mark Twain said the two most important days in every person's life are "the day they are born, and the day they figure out WHY!'"

It   sounds   easy,   but   our   WHY   is   often overlooked in transition. One big reason is that we are so aligned with our WHY when we are serving in the military that we aren't even conscious of it when we leave.

We just think it will follow us down to Main Street America, don't we? Nope.

To leverage our higher purpose like we did in the military, we have to actively reconnect with it, rediscover it, and be mindful in bringing it with us through transition.

The life we lead as warriors is often the ultimate manifestation of serving something bigger than ourselves. But it's not all that we are.

HIGH PERFORMANCE IS A WAY OF LIFE FOR YOU

Most warriors are high performers. To follow this notion of service above self, you have to be. The focus and dedication needed to achieve the near-impossible feats that are everyday requirements in today's military, mandate that you perform at a hyperoptimal level of purpose-based function.

This high-performance approach is more than a mindset. It's coursing through your veins and embedded in your DNA. It's just who you are, baby!

High performers have a unique ability to operate at different thresholds. One moment, you can employ the lethality of the Grim Reaper in a close fight involving grenades and bare hands. The next, you demonstrate deep people skills as you listen patiently to a tribal elder describe his family lineage.

We can turn these various levels on and off like

a light switch, can't we? It's what makes us strategic — and what distinguishes us as military professionals.

What we can't turn on and off is the inner purpose that drives us toward service above self. That shit stays with you, but that purpose has to be fed. These realities — this purpose — must be redirected into other things.

WHAT UNCLE SAM DOESN'T GET TO KEEP

When it's time to leave the military, that higher purpose often is left behind. It flowed so naturally in uniform but it is no longer as intuitive as it once was. That can start to gnaw at us as we take that high-paying sales manager job, because we think that's what society wants us to do.

Look, I am not hating on new jobs or minimizing any form of employment. But regardless of what you do for a living, your higher purpose can't be ignored.

The fact is many of us shut off the light in our squad bay for the last time and leave that purpose behind us. Or at least we try to. But it'll find you, and sometimes on ugly terms.

Your higher purpose is not the property of Uncle Sam. That's not part of government equipment issue that gets turned back in during out-processing. Your WHY is yours, and it's one of your greatest assets in transition. Make sure you identify it and keep it front and center.

What if we don't do this? Well, unfortunately, I see this way too often in veterans coming into the civilian side. We ignore the power of purpose at our peril. Ignoring our inner purpose when we leave the military is a good bet we won't live the post-service life we were meant to live (at best) and an open invitation for a snakes-in-the-head house party (at worst).

This disconnection from our purpose is at the heart of the severe transition issues facing our warriors, ranging from suicide to marital strain.

12

TRUE NORTH

Crickets.

I testified to the House Armed Services Committee on the challenges surrounding military transition. I spoke honestly and candidly about many of the topics in this book, above all the issue of redirecting the warrior purpose to something else as being the singular shortfall facing our veterans today.

I am not sure what the assembled group of politicians and senior military leaders expected to hear from me, but you could have heard crickets chirping when I was done talking.

I wish I could describe the look on the faces of Marine Corps and Army general officers sitting near me as I spoke about this issue. I honestly don't think they had ever heard this perspective regarding transition.

Higher purpose? Sense of self? Redirection?

They seemed very uncomfortable with it.

WHAT WE DON'T TALK ABOUT HURTS US THE MOST

Unfortunately, when service members and veterans start talking about fulfillment, happiness, higher purpose, prosperity or other perceived "leaf-eating" terms, our "carnivore" mindset gets a little uneasy.

One thing I've noticed since working with hundreds of transitioning veterans is that it's often the very senior generals, admirals, colonels, master chiefs, and sergeants major that have the hardest time getting out of their own way and finding their higher purpose that fulfills them after the military. If this is you, stop believing your own press from your time in service and get back to what really makes you tick.

If this talk seems a little touchy-feely to you, I hope you find a way through it. But wait, we have to maintain the 'warrior' image. If it doesn't suck, it isn't worth doing. Right?

Bullshit. We have to change this paradigm when going into the real world. We need to redirect our purpose.

Redirecting our purpose from the military life to a life in the civilian world has less to do with seeing how much misery you can endure (which is what military training has hardwired many of us to do), and much more to do with finding what lights you up — what makes you happy.

One reason this process is so difficult is because we have to look deeply at ourselves — not always pleasant in our line of work, is it? Redirection of your purpose starts with clarity and self-awareness. Without it, we are lost.

GETTING OUT OF OUR OWN WAY

"People have life targets they want to get to, but if you do not know where you are, then how can you get to the place you are keen to get to?" asked Anil Gupta, author of *Immediate Happiness*, when talking to a group of transitioning veterans. "And how do you know whether that is what you are truly seeking?"

Here is something no one else is going to tell you in transition: You must give yourself the opportunity to reflect on who you are — on what drives you. Without this, you will be incomplete. Don't worry about what your peers think about this, or how you'll be viewed in "warrior court."

This is about **you**.

Do the work and spend time on this. You have to get out of your own way and give it the attention it deserves. Only after you have the clarity of your "true north" on your life's compass should you start to think about what your transition goals should be.

TRY THIS AS ONE WAY TO GET CLEAR ON YOUR PURPOSE:

Go someplace quiet with a pen and paper. (No interruptions allowed.)

Close your eyes and think back to the day you first came into the military. Chaos, right? Trash cans bouncing down the hall at zero-dark-thirty. Your drill instructor is screaming in your face as his spittle hits your cheek. You are doing so many pushups that you are about to throw up. Part of you is scared shitless, yet inwardly part of you is smiling.

What the hell is the matter with you?

Were you crazy? What were you thinking? How could you have been excited about this? What in the hell made you sign on for this kind of life?

Even if you hated the military life, you still felt some kind of crazy pride in what you were doing, didn't you? What was it? A sense of honor? The brotherhood or sisterhood of service? Adrenaline? A sense of adventure?

Whatever it was...write it down.

Now think back to the worst day you had in the military. Maybe it's the day you buried your best friend. Maybe it was a bad firefight. Maybe you just got in trouble at work.

But when all the logic in your mind and body was telling you to leave the service — to grow your hair out, smoke dope, and play Xbox, what force held your feet in place? What compelled you to stay, despite your better judgment? Loyalty to your unit? Was it a commitment to your brother and sister warriors? Even if it was fear of the outside world that held you in place, write it down.

Now fast-forward 15 years or so. Your little granddaughter is sitting on your lap. She looks up at you with those big eyes and asks you, "Granddad, what was it like? What was it like in those places you served? What were your friends like that you served with? I see you talking to them sometimes when you think you're alone — and you seem sad. What was it like?"

What are you going to tell her?

Write it down.

WHAT IT ALL MEANS

You see, the answer to those questions...things like making a difference bigger than yourself, patriotism, loyalty — those are the components of not just your warrior ethos, but your design as a human being.

Those don't belong to the military. They belong to you.

They define who you are. They define your purpose.

They don't go away just because you take off the uniform and leave the military. That's who you are.

Take those answers and craft a one-sentence purpose for yourself — and keep working on it.

Maybe it would help to know my purpose.

My purpose is to help other people leave their tracks for serving others in this world.

My father impressed this on me at a young age. I honed those skills in the military, and I am doing it as a speaker on stages and civilian leadership workshops today.

What's yours?

I am giving you permission right now to reconnect to that purpose that defines you as a warrior and redirect it into the next phase of your life.

I am counting on you to do this. No matter what occupation you choose after military service; where you live; or how much money you make…this internal rediscovery of your higher purpose is the only way you'll be truly happy and live the life of prosperity you and your loved ones so richly deserve.

Now let's look at the enemy who will try to stop you!

13

MEDIOCRITY SUCKS

NEW YORK CITY, 2013

"Finding higher purpose sounds great — but I have to feed my family. This is the real world." Some of you might push back on redirecting your passion.

I've heard this before. I get it.

Sometimes you have to take what you can get to put food on the table. That's just how it goes.

REALITY CHECK

Think about this, though: Did you get exactly what you wanted when you joined the military? Or did you have to work hard and pay your dues over time to get where you wanted to be? Did success come overnight, or did you have to grind it out in the afterhours when everyone else was asleep in their rack?

How can we expect civilian life to be any different?

Even if you take that customer service job or part-time employment to meet your immediate needs, don't give up on your higher purpose.

You'll regret it if you do.

WHY PURPOSE MATTERS

If you go into a line of work you don't like, even for a long period, you don't have to leave your warrior ethos behind.

More often than not, though, this is exactly what happens. Then things start to unravel.

There are other ways to redirect your purpose. I know plenty of happy veterans who don't just limit their purpose-driven thinking to professional life.

"I'm happiest when I'm helping other guys navigate the VA medical system that kicked my ass." This is what Tom, a Vietnam veteran, told me about why he volunteers outside of his day job to help veterans get their health benefits.

Go back to the gaps left in your life from leaving the military. What do you miss most? It might be the adventure. It might be the outdoors. It might be giving back to something bigger than yourself. Maybe you need to volunteer — or start your own nonprofit. (This helped me immensely, and still does. I feel connected to my military brothers and sisters by my nonprofit work to assist them in transition.) But it doesn't have to be some noble volunteer cause.

Maybe it's picking up a challenging fitness program that gets you back into the game of life. Maybe it's taking on a new hobby you've always wanted to do. My brother learned to fly when he got out of the Army.

Perhaps it's focusing on your kids as a stay-at-home dad in a way that you couldn't or didn't do in the military. Chad Tucker, former Marine pilot, is doing this with the same gusto and determination he used to land on carrier decks in the middle of the night.

There are also nonprofits like Team RUBICON that help adrenaline junkies like you and me get involved as volunteers in rough areas of the world during catastrophe and crisis. The point is this — fight to keep your purpose at the center of your life whether it's professionally, personally, or both.

A word about combat contracting. A lot of our community does this. They simply switch out their body armor vests, grow their hair a bit longer, and go to work for a company down-range advising or even gunfighting. A word of caution:

If you do this, because you just love the action or you need to carve some space out in your life to save money and then make your next move, no worries — go get 'em.

But if you are doing this work because you think it's all you are capable of doing or that you don't have the time to chase your dreams, I want you to rethink this move.

IT'S TIME TO INCLUDE YOUR DREAMS

Sergeant Major Bill was all set to retire. He was hanging up his jungle boots after a quarter century of service, much of it as a special operator in combat.

He had a good-paying job as a contractor shortly after retirement. He had plenty of money and more time at home than ever before. Still, something was missing.

He started to go through depression. "I was in some dark places," Bill told me. "Even though I was around the military guys, it was nothing like being in the service. Finally, I realized that I needed to find a way to find that higher purpose I felt when I was in Special Ops."

Bill started volunteering to mentor other guys in transition. Nothing formal, he just made himself available in whatever way made sense at the moment. Bingo!

That slight shift scratched the deep itch that was leaving gaps in his *new normal*. That's why it's important to consider all aspects of your life for redirection of purpose. These include recreation, self-improvement, and other mind-body-spirit opportunities that make you whole and give you the fulfillment and peace you want and deserve after all those years of service.

You won't get a better time than right now. Even if you are already out of the service, think broadly about what's missing from your post-military life, and how you can fill it across every aspect of your new journey.

This will take some work. No one will encourage you to do this. The train won't slow down for you to find new dreams. If you are still serving, Operational Tempo (OPTEMPO) will increase. Deployments will take you away. Family events will beckon. Your chain of command will want more from you than ever.

If you are already out of the military, you'll have to answer the demands of job, family, etc., while fighting like hell to identify and protect your purpose.

However you decide to do it — just do it. Find time to identify your higher purpose. Otherwise, life will sneak up on you like an insider threat in an Afghan base camp, and you'll be forced to settle, or worse — the snakes will start to slither. And that just sucks.

FINDING THE PATH...

What if you can't find what you are passionate about as the reality of transition creeps ever closer? That can be scary as hell, right? I felt that as the date of transition came at me like a freight train.

Well, slow down just a bit. Take a breath.

Passions come and go. Locating your higher purpose is essential.

You have quite a few warrior attributes that can fill this void until a new passion emerges. Most specifically, regimen, discipline, and rigor are massive assets. The application of discipline in the fog of transition uncertainy is one of the greatest ways to open up opportunities you never even thought of.

For the first year after Army retirement, I really didn't know what to do. So I did a lot of things. They ranged from government contracting to writing my book. It was frustrating as I struggled to find a passion that rivaled my military service. Then I found it.

I discovered public speaking, and in that, a new path for my life. But it wasn't the many jobs I tried out that led me there. Rather, it was my focused routine on physical training, health, and inward reflection that ultimately led me to that path.

Discipline of your day toward your mind, body, and spirit is the ultimate tool for discovering your passion.

Mission America tip: Two great books I recommend to you for building this resilience early on are *The War of Art* and *Turning Pro* by Steven Pressfield. These books are essential companions to finding the essence of your life's work after the military. They also help you fight the snakes that may try to derail you in the process.

"Dude, I don't have time for this shit," the transitioning sergeant, whom I'll call Z, told me as we talked about his plan. "I gotta find a job…and quick."

Too often — in transition — our military community settles for what they think our society wants them to do, instead of being who they are. This is seriously dangerous. Let me go deeper here.

DON'T SETTLE

There are three specific cautions associated with not redirecting our purpose and instead settling for whatever comes along.

First, it creates an unclear path for you. You will become exhausted. Settling places obstacles in your path. It leaves you to bumble aimlessly along, "figuring it out" while grasping at shiny objects that don't support your higher purpose.

Second, settling puts your overall health and wellness at risk. Not redirecting your passion makes you vulnerable to the enemies of resilience. You endured the corrosive elements of combat with varying degrees of success. You found a way to push the snakes in your head down below the surface in order to go on another deployment.

You pursued rigorous physical regimens — in spite of injuries — to keep up with your teammates. You stayed mentally sharp in your professional pursuits, ranging from training schools to professional reading lists. You were able to roll with whatever life threw at you, largely because your goals motivated you to do that. Now what?

When you run counter to your purpose, the resilience you built as a warrior ebbs away. The snakes come out to play. They see the opening, and shoot a gap straight for your exposed soul.

Your desire for maintaining fitness fades. Your spirit for staying mentally sharp dulls under the mind-numbing aspect of settling into what you think life is "supposed" to be or what you are "supposed" to do. And then, life starts kicking your ass in ways you can't even describe to other people who never served.

Third, settling denies your unique contributions to civil society, namely cheating America out of much-needed leadership.

In case you haven't noticed, America isn't in great shape these days. In fact, she's hurting pretty bad. The economy is lagging and jobs are in low supply, but more importantly, our collective character doesn't seem to shine as bright as it once did. This is a leadership deficit.

The skills and experience you used to make a strategic difference in Afghanistan, Iraq, Colombia, and the Philippines could make an equally big impact at home. Do you believe that?

It's true. I've had numerous opportunities to make a difference in society since retirement. These opportunities abound, but if you simply settle for whatever life hands you, your eyes will be closed to them.

And what about all the veterans coming behind you? They are going to face the same challenges you did. Maybe worse. Who will help them find their path, if not you? No one else is coming. DOD won't do it. The VA won't get it done. The corporate world can't pull this off no matter how many hiring programs they sponsor. It's up to us (you and me) to look after our own.

Think back to the most basic warrior ethos you

learned at a young age in the military — taking care of your battle buddy. If you're just trudging along, head down, sweat dripping off your nose as you gut out the never-ending road march of life, with no inner purpose guiding your steps, you won't be there when your teammates move toward their transition goals.

That would be a shame. My post-retirement work has found those efforts — of giving back to the warriors coming behind me — to be some of the most meaningful redirection activities of all.

You would think this purpose-based transition to be very instinctive. You don't need anyone telling you to do that. This is not something you're going to overlook in transition. You know who you are and what you want.

Yet I see warriors do it time and again, every day. I think it's at the heart of many veteran social challenges like suicide, substance abuse, depression, and just plain detaching from society and giving up on your dreams.

You might think you are not worthy of chasing your dreams. "This is a self-indulgent fantasy," you might say. Or, "I'd like to do this, man, but transition is coming too fast," the practical mind cautions. Or how about this one? "There is no time for touchy-feely things like this. It's too risky. I need to just do what I can to stay afloat." I hear these comments a lot from warriors just like you all the time, regardless of service.

By not doing this, the danger is that you underestimate the significance of that higher purpose in who you are and what you do. It is essential to defining your emerging identity.

FINDING PURPOSE REQUIRES INTENTION

That purpose that has driven you for so long, that has influenced your personal and professional decisions and relationships all these years, is the first thing left in the corner when you turn the light off in the squad bay and start your civilian journey.

You are a warrior. Carrying the warrior ethos with you is critical. You must have complete self-awareness of who you are, how you are hardwired, and the purpose that drives you.

This brings those post-service life objectives into crisp focus much quicker as you're walking down the path of transition — even if you haven't chosen the goal yet.

You might bounce around a little bit as you figure it out. That's OK, as long as you maintain your internal regimen throughout those uncertain times. Hold tight to who you are and what you stand for. The answers will come through exporting the self-discipline you had in the military.

14

MANAGING EXPECTATIONS

RIVERVIEW, FLORIDA, 2015

"I feel like I am just spinning my wheels," he said as he stirred his fork over and over in his scrambled eggs. I was having breakfast with Chris, a recently retired Army officer. "Nothing is like what I expected it to be in the civilian world. My wife and kids are just as frustrated as I am. I never thought I'd miss the Army, but I do."

EXPECTATION MANAGEMENT

There are three really important things about managing expectations in transition:

First (steel yourself for this one), you may have to work really hard to find something that equates to what you did in military service. Sorry. It's just hard to replicate that environment. Even toting a gun as a contractor probably won't cut it.

That's because the life of a warrior is an honor-based occupation built around <u>team</u> and <u>service</u> that is unlike any organization in the world. You are transitioning from a group-centric honor society into an individual-focused, transactional world that often values achievement over all else.

mean you won't find a level of happiness and prosperity that exceeds your time in service. In fact, the lessons in this book are designed to help you do just that.

Second, transition takes time. It can take a lot of time. How much, varies from person to person. Think back to the military, and how long it took to achieve big goals. Did you hit your stride right out of basic training? Did you say to yourself, "I've arrived," after you pinned on your E-5 stripes?

Of course not.

It took time to find your military mojo. This process will too.

Third, nothing is free. NOTHING!

It might feel like it, but resist this feeling. You will hear me say this a lot. Sure, I know, there are all the touching commercials and multimillion-dollar initiatives to hire tens of thousands of vets, but make no mistake, nothing in life is free.

And if it is, I recommend you proceed with caution. Here is why: You are a high performer who has built a life around grinding out strategic results from resource-scarce situations. This adaptive mindset is one of the greatest transition assets in your kit bag.

Was anything handed to you in the military, other than a weapon and a heavy pack? Did anyone say to you, "Hey man, just sit back and relax…we're going to sort this out for you. It's OK, you've earned it." Hell no!

You had to work for everything you got. Nothing has changed in transition.

Well, it should make your skin crawl if anyone makes similar promises regarding anything being free in the civilian world.

Even the programs that offer free services to veterans to help them transition — and there are some great ones — shouldn't be considered free. Patriotic civilians wrote a lot of checks and donated a lot of hours to make these products possible.

These veteran transition initiatives, like the ones on the American Dream U website, are valuable resources. But you must invest the effort. If you're not going to do that, then don't bother. Time and sweat equity, as you'll continue to discover, are two of your most precious natural resources — and the only ones that can't be replaced.

I've seen too many active duty members and family members pass on transition preparation opportunities because they aren't free. This is a mistake. If it gets you where you want to go, faster and more effectively than doing it on your own, and it resonates with you…do it, even if you have to invest in it.

IT STARTS WITH YOU

Take the time during transition to invest in yourself, your loved ones, and your dreams in order to prepare for your transition.

This bad narrative of our civilian population fixing your transition problems, or owing you a job, is misguided at best, and dangerous at worst. If you buy into an entitlement mentality like this, it will neuter you from 'crushing it' as the high-performing problem solver you were meant to be.

I'm not saying you shouldn't accept the generosity of our civilian communities. By all means, make use of them. But treat every program, every training event, and every product as a strategic asset. **Don't ever think you are entitled to anything in life other than the sweat on your brow — another great military lesson to take to your grave.**

No one knows that more than a warrior. It's this ethos that you need to maintain so that you don't check out of the game, which is the subject of our next chapter.

15

DON'T CHECK OUT

Frozen.

I was frozen.

"Scott, Eric is dead."

It was Eric's mother-in-law on the other end of the line. I could hear Elizabeth's words, but my mind kept telling me it wasn't real.

But it was real.

Sergeant Eric Landon, just days before deploying to yet another remote duty station, killed himself — leaving behind a beautiful young wife, and two little girls under the age of three.

I had seen Eric a few weeks back. He seemed upbeat and engaged.

I had missed it. We all had.

Eric wasn't the first warrior friend I've lost to suicide. He was, in fact, the fourth.

I want him to be the last.

This has to stop.

UNACCEPTABLE LOSS

We are losing far too many brother and sister warriors to suicide today. One is too many, but in the last few years the numbers have climbed to as high as 22 veterans and one active duty soldier per day. This is far above the national average for suicide.

Even our sworn enemy, the Islamic State, is exploiting this social challenge by highlighting veteran suicide in their recent propaganda video entitled "No Respite." Our suicides are giving propaganda rocket fuel to the most dangerous enemy our country faces.

If you are in that space of crisis and you are thinking about suicide, DON'T DO IT. We need you around.

I need you around.

OFF THE GRID

And what about just going off the grid? You know what I am talking about. Just disappearing into the sunset and isolating yourself. Or maybe, your way of coping with transition is to go off on your own and self-medicate with booze, pills, or both.

If you are thinking about checking out in any of these ways, don't, OK? Here's why.

You didn't run all those miles…endure all the hardships…earn all those scars, and get scuffed up like you have, just to fade away.

Fuck that.

There is a bigger plan for you, so let's figure out what it is — one day at a time.

Instead, if you are in a crisis as a veteran or veteran family member, call 1-800-273-8255.

You can also visit the Stop Suicide Soldier website at www.stopsoldiersuicide.org.

OUT OF THE DARKNESS

"I really believed I was the Grim Reaper," an active duty warrant officer I'll call Mike confided quietly to the assembled crowd of veterans and small business owners. "Based on the stuff I'd done and seen in combat, I was having serious issues dealing with it."

Mike was a highly decorated combat veteran, a Silver Star winner. He also self-identified with post-traumatic stress disorder (PTSD) and sought out treatment within the Special Operations community. That was 2008.

Today, he's a different man.

Still on active duty and still deploying, Mike now describes himself as happy and healthy. Although there was once heavy strain on his family relationships, they are once again strong and intact. I've known Mike for several years. He's always been an amazing leader, but he is performing at a much higher level than he was in '08, when the challenges of combat reared their ugly head in his life.

For many of you, internal injuries, like PTSD and traumatic brain injury (TBI), will eat your lunch. There are still lots of things we don't understand about these grievous injuries, but what we do know is that they are rampant in this military population. If left untended, they can be a major contributor in all sorts of post-service issues, including veteran suicide and depression.

WHAT'S OUT THERE

There are a growing number of nonprofit initiatives committed to tackling the issue of PTSD and TBI.

There are some really exciting breakthroughs in this field that offer hope to even the most severely affected veterans. For example, Doctor Diego Hernandez has done tremendous work with veterans dealing with these issues.

There are scores of opportunities to address these challenges that you or a loved one might be experiencing from combat or transition stress. There are even scholarships available for the ART therapy programs that Doc Diego offers to military members through the Camaraderiefoundation.org.

If you're looking to get involved on veteran issues, this is a great place to do it. Contact Mission America and we'll help you connect to some outstanding nonprofit organizations that are tackling the veteran crisis issues.

LOOKING OUT FOR EACH OTHER

What else can be done? Well, how about we look out for each other?

If you are former or active military, you are often going to see the signs of suicide, depression, and other post-service resilience issues in our warriors before anyone else.

Often these are your former battle buddies and teammates. We have to stay in touch with each other. We have to look each other in the eye from time to time and say, "You OK, man?"

I know that sounds immensely simple, but when I think of the friends I've lost to suicide, alcoholism, and other post-service issues, I believe I could have done a better job of connecting with them and picking up on the signs. I am much more vigilant about this now than I've ever been before, and I'm asking you to do the same.

There are also intervention groups in communities throughout the country and plenty of places for you to donate your time and money at a very grassroots level. Any cause that tackles the mental disorders caused by combat is a worthwhile endeavor to citizens looking to help warriors come home.

I recently attended a training session on suicide and PTSD taught by Sheriff Timothy Whitcomb of Cattaraugus County, New York. His unique perspective as a mental health expert, educator, and law enforcement officer who has seen the ugly side of traumatic stress and suicide gave me a lot of insight, and one piece I'll share with you here.

Whitcomb stated to a room full of senior law enforcement officers that **PTSD is the only mental disorder that is 100 percent manageable and treatable.**

This is also great news for patriotic Americans looking to make an impact on veterans issues, and a small community of warriors who've seen a lot of combat but who are ready to get into the game and lead our communities. Let's work together with our citizens and crush this snake once and for all — our communities and our nation are counting on it.

Now that we've addressed the broad aspects of mindset in transition, let's look at some critical skills that you won't get anywhere else.

PART II
SKILL SET FOR TRANSITION

16

LEAD WITH STORY

"The most powerful person in the world is the storyteller."
— Steve Jobs

JOINT BASE LEWIS-MCCHORD, WASHINGTON, 2014

We were like statues.

No one moved as he talked. I was teaching a negotiations course to Army soldiers in Fort Lewis, Washington. The focus was on using negotiations when talking to potential employers and investors.

But at this moment I was the student, along with every other soldier in the crowded classroom as the staff sergeant, whom I'll call William, recalled the most hellish day his platoon ever endured in the mean streets of Fallujah, Iraq in 2006.

I had just asked for a volunteer from the audience to talk about the greatest leadership challenge they faced in combat and how they overcame it. The point of this exercise was not for a "No shit, there I was" story (although those are irresistibly fun among us warrior types), but rather as an example of how story can differentiate us from every other fish in the pond.

It had been a seriously shitty day for William and his infantry platoon. They had been chopped to shreds in an ambush that included improvised explosives and machine-gun fire. Suffering multiple killed in action and even more wounded in action, his platoon was 40 percent disabled within minutes of the attack initiation. But that wasn't the most compelling part of the story.

It was how he led after the attack that held us all motionless.

This man embodied leadership skill, empathy, and personal connection that all employers, lenders, and academic institutions look for in human resources and investment potential.

This amazing non-commissioned officer used these powerful leader qualities to inspire his men to put their horrific losses behind them, overcome their reservations, and get back into the fight for another mission, just hours later.

This was raw leadership on display. All I could think about as I heard this amazing story of warrior leadership was how much any employer on the planet would love to have this guy leading her people.

When Staff Sergeant William finished telling that story, the whole room, including me, was emotionally locked into him. They were ready to follow him wherever he went.

I gathered my thoughts and said, "OK, guys — this is what I mean. This is the perfect example of the type of story that will bowl civilians over — whether you are asking for a job, a loan, or looking to be admitted into a prestigious college. Great job,

William."

As I moved away from him to continue my talk, his hand slowly went back up. "Uh, excuse me sir," he said sheepishly, "I haven't told that story in any of my job interviews, I usually just give them my résumé and try to stick to their questions."

Holy shit!

We are selling ourselves short here. I see this everywhere in our community. Let's unpack it.

YOUR UNTAPPED TRANSITION ASSET — YOUR STORY

Our warrior ethos is phenomenal for transition. However, our concept of training, honor, and humility, in this case, is unhelpful if it's preventing us from telling the personal stories that convey our past as warriors. This is especially true if these stories are relevant to the world we're returning to.

Redirecting your purpose is the most important component of your Mission America *mindset*. But telling your personal story is the most important Mission America *skill set*.

As you take stock of what you need to take with you after military service, know this: Your story is your greatest asset in transition!

STORY AND JOB INTERVIEWS

"If I am running the job interview, I would rather hear the story of a warrior any day than read the endless line of dry résumés from Ivy League college kids with no life experience or leadership skills," said Phil Randazzo to the group of assembled Army soldiers.

Phil should know. As a highly accomplished real estate entrepreneur and CEO of the nonprofit

American Dream U, which trains thousands of veterans in all kinds of entrepreneurial skills, he has seen thousands of résumés from all types of potential employees.

Mission America tip: American Dream U is an amazing resource for veterans and their families who are up against transition. Phil is tied into some of the most successful entrepreneurs on the planet. These gals and guys are real patriots who will share their best practices with you in person at VETRACON events as American Dream U travels base to base, as well as in all kinds of virtual learning programs at AmericanDreamU.org.

I've seen this training firsthand as I've presented on Phil's stage, and as I've trained warriors and military family members in the audience. No matter where you are in transition — active duty, reservist, or already out of service — I personally endorse and recommend American Dream U as a critical partner in your transition team room. Now, back to story.

I've used storytelling in every aspect of my Special Forces and civilian life, and the results are always strategic. Whether it's closing on multimillion-dollar real estate deals or raising money for wounded veterans, telling a story is the most effective way to differentiate yourself as an authentic, capable leader.

WHY STORY WORKS

Think about this:

Storytelling is the oldest form of communication in the world and is still the most powerful. "Our brain is hardwired to respond to story," writes Lisa Cron in her book, *Wired for Story*.

"It teaches us the way of the world."

It seems hard to believe in this age of hyper-connectivity, sound bites, and communicating in 140 characters or less…but it's true.

How influential is story in today's business world? *Harvard Business Review* called story a strategic tool with "irresistible power" and it was labeled "the major business lesson of 2014" by *Entrepreneur Magazine.*

Story has a massive impact on potential employers, lenders, academic institutions, and a range of other audiences. "Stories encapsulate, into one compact package, information, knowledge, context, and emotion," says Don Norman, author of *Things That Make Us Smart.*

And guess what? If you are an American warrior, past or present, odds are that you have some badass stories that can make a big difference in how you live the rest of your life and the purpose you attain.

Your stories provide meaning. "They ignite the region of the brain that processes meaning," says cultural anthropologist Michael Wesch. "Humans are meaning-seeking creatures. We can't remember anything without giving meaning to it."

That means purposeful stories told by you to lenders, employers, and even your family members will stick to their bones much more than the

hundreds of résumés, personal bios, job applications, and talking points they hear throughout the day.

HOW STORIES CAN SERVE YOU IN TRANSITION

This is where the art and science of storytelling can serve you in the civilian world.

Stories connect us to people in ways that are lasting and deep, through empathy and reciprocity. When we listened to Staff Sergeant William talk about that fateful day, we were connected the same way tribesmen gathered around a fire were connected 10,000 years ago to a storyteller describing life-saving lessons to his clan that he learned on the day's hunt.

We could feel what he was feeling. That is empathy. As he made himself more and more relatable to us, we moved toward a feeling of reciprocity. This is where we felt compelled to do something for him. This isn't manipulative. This is how humans are hardwired to connect and do transactions — through storytelling.

In fact, the reward centers of our brain that have driven human behavior for 200,000 years love storytelling. The neuroeconomist Paul Zak has conducted numerous studies that show good storytelling results in emissions of the molecule oxytocin, which promotes trustworthiness.

These same studies have shown that people even donated more money to charity when told compelling stories instead of hearing dry presentations or 'death by PowerPoint.'

As world-famous movie producer and multimillion-dollar dealmaker Peter Guber writes in his must-read book *Tell to Win*, "Move their hearts and their feet and wallet will follow."

As powerful as story potentially is in your transition, there is a challenge that you have to overcome: it's the same one that kept Staff Sergeant William from telling his leadership story to potential employers.

GETTING OUT OF YOUR OWN WAY — PART II

You struggle to talk about yourself. You're not alone. We warriors are conditioned NOT to talk about ourselves. Think about it. Your entire military career, you have been conditioned to be a quiet professional; to not talk about yourself. This often carries over into civilian life.

The notion of the quiet professional is admirable, but it should not prevent you from telling powerful stories that help you serve others and reach your higher purpose in your life beyond the military.

Obviously, I am not advocating self-serving actions or revealing sensitive information. You are intuitive enough to easily tell the difference. But telling stories about the miles you've run, the lessons you have learned, and how your leadership skills can have an impact on our civilian society or the workplace are essential tools in your kit bag.

THE HEALING POWER OF STORIES

Stories also help us on the inside.

"Stories heal the brain," says Dr. Joan Rosenberg, world-renowned mental health professional and Air Force veteran. "As long as stories are told by veterans in the service of healing and helping others, even stories of trauma can bring hurting warriors into the light," she concludes.

In fact, according to studies by Dr. Richard Tedechi and Dr. Lawrence Calhoun, highlighted in Carmine Gallo's book *The Storyteller's Secret*, "Many people have learned how to reframe traumatic events into meaning and purpose in their lives."

They do this by bringing their stories out of their head and into the world. The same possibility holds true for you, no matter what dark valleys you've been through. I invite you to try it.

One word of caution: If you are developing your personal story and there is trauma in your past, make sure to work with a mental health professional in your unit or community. At the very least, advise them of your plan for story development and get their insight on how to best proceed. It's different for everyone, but so important to your transition capacity. Doc Diego is a Mission America resource you can reach out to in order to make this connection.

Mission America tip: *Try this* — write your warrior's story.

Have you ever heard of the *Hero's Journey*? It's an ancient story format that is present in almost every story, from the tale of King Arthur to *Rocky*. It goes something like this:

Departure: Our warrior (that's you, by the way) hears a call. Refuses it at first, and then crosses over the great divide into a new world.

Initiation: Our warrior faces tough challenges. Stares into the abyss. Along the way, usually with the help of some mentors who give the hero a divine gift, he transforms and assumes a new perspective in life.

Return: Our warrior returns home now, the master of two worlds and committed to improving each of them. This is where you can make it crystal-clear that your evolution as a warrior makes you the optimal choice for the job, the loan, or entry into a school.

Now take that framework of the Hero's Journey and develop your personal story of your time as a warrior. Imagine the impact that could have to a future employer or lender. Tell your story strongly enough that this person sees the answer to their problem in your story.

That's the kind of leader society deserves and your personal story can ensure this happens.

OR, TRY THIS:

Go somewhere quiet with a pen and pad.

Reflect on the most decisive leadership challenge you had while in the military. Summarize it in a single sentence and write it down.

Now build a story around how that moment shaped you as a leader and how those events, experience, and skills position you as the kind of leader that can make a difference in whatever civilian endeavor you are about to do.

HERE IS ONE MORE THING YOU CAN DO WITH STORY:

Storytelling is also about listening and empathy. Learn everything you can about your interviewer, the company you are applying to, the bank you are asking for a loan. Tell your story in a way that ends with a compelling narrative of how your life as a warrior can overcome the pain points or maximize the opportunities of the person or organization you're trying to connect with.

RESOURCES

I recommend three books on story. First, as mentioned above, read *Tell to Win* by Peter Guber.

It's a great book on the power and techniques of storytelling. Second, read *The Hero with a Thousand Faces* by Joseph Campbell. It can help you construct your personal story as a warrior into the framework of the Hero's Journey. Third, I recommend *The Storyteller's Secret* by Carmine Gallo, also mentioned earlier. This book is chock full of great tips on how to tell the most compelling stories with the biggest impact.

Here is another cool resource: If you are developing your personal story, I've created a free video only for warriors and warrior families. It's on our Mission America website (therealmissionamerica.org) under 'Resources.' It's password protected but worth your time.

Now that you've developed your story, what about telling it? This is a skill in itself.

How you deliver your story, how you present your employment pitch, and how you connect with the relevant people in your new world is essential. There is no better coach than former NFL football legend and international presence, Bo Eason. He's my coach and I recommend you check him out.

There are so many ways to use story in your life after service. A resume is still important, but trust me — the potential value from the stories in your Mission America arsenal is limitless. The more you can identify these stories, and tell them in an impactful way, the more likely you are to achieve the purpose you were meant to achieve.

Our transition compass of redirected purpose and personal stories are powerful skills. Now we need to muster another great asset — the new members of our team...

Our transition tribe.

17

BUILDING YOUR TRANSITION 'TEAM ROOM'

FORT BRAGG, NORTH CAROLINA, 1997

When I was a brand-new captain assigned to 7th Special Forces Group, my detachment was notified of an upcoming deployment to Colombia. This was going to be a complicated counterdrug mission working with the U.S. embassy and various Colombian security forces.

I had never deployed with my team before. I figured there was no time like the present to step up and assert my 'commander role.' In preparation for the upcoming mission, I gathered my senior team members and gave out what I thought was high-impact planning guidance.

Wrong-o.

My team sergeant, Mike (God bless him for his patience with me), politely held up his hand. "Sir, how about this?" he said with his soft-spoken voice.

"Let's walk down the hall and talk to the team in Charlie Company that just got back from Colombia. Once they give us a baseline understanding of reality, then you can tell us how you'd like the mission to go. Sound fair?"

Within minutes we were sitting in the other detachment's team room. The other team was in a circle as they spoke openly with my warrant officer, my team sergeant, and me. Each of them, starting with the other team's captain, gave his perspective on the mission, what he did wrong, right, and what he would recommend we do differently. The medic, the weapons guy, the intelligence sergeant...all did the same thing. It was incredible.

When we left that team room all three of us had a much more comprehensive understanding of how to prepare for this mission than I had ever thought possible. In the coming days, the rest of our team would visit this team room and pair up with their counterparts for additional technical information.

I learned a lesson that day I would never forget that still serves me today — and it can serve you in transition.

This is the power of the 'team room.' Every unit, in every branch of service, has its version of the team room: a squad bay, a ready room, etc.

THE COLLABORATIVE POWER OF YOUR TEAM ROOM

Regardless of what you call it in your branch of service, it's the place where you go to get the real 'skinny' on what's going on, or to learn the latest about places where we're going from those who've already been there. It's where we pool our resources and collaborate to get shit done. It's a place to identify problems, to plan, to connect, and to collaborate.

So tell me this: Why in the hell does the most collaborative and team-oriented organization on the planet — the U.S. military — completely abandon this approach when it's time for one of us to walk away and leave the service?

GOING AGAINST OUR NATURE

Why do you go off on your own to take on a transition mission you have never seen before?

In a recent talk I gave at Fort Bragg to a group of Green Berets, I asked, "How many of you speak at least once a month to one or more of your buddies who have retired or transitioned recently?"

Out of about 30 people, only two or three hands went up. I've asked that same question to active duty service members around the country and always get the same response. Almost none.

You need to stay in touch with guys and gals as they leave your unit into the civilian world. It can dramatically reduce your transition learning curve.

I also ask warriors, when I'm training them, how many of them are actively reaching out to relevant civilian leaders who hold knowledge, resources, or access to the things they'd like to do after service. Almost no hands go up.

As a military community, we're not doing a good job of connecting with relevant players on our new journey. Instead we turn the light off in the 'team room' when we take off the uniform and never really turn it back on. Why?

I need you to change this.

I want you to keep the lights on in your team

room. But here's the thing. It won't be the same teammates. It's going to fill up with new mentors, new peers, and resource leaders. That's OK. It's the process I need you to trust.

STRETCHING COMFORT ZONES...

The process for team building and gaining insight into new situations is exactly the same as the team room Mike took us to before deploying to Colombia. You just need to stretch your comfort zone and bring in new teammates. Let's look at a real-world example on the civilian side.

When my brother Travis (also a veteran) and I decided we wanted to go into real estate, we selected manufactured housing communities... yeah, yeah, trailer parks. It was the right asset class and passive income for what we wanted to do. But we knew almost nothing about it.

Still on active duty, this is when we turned the light on in a new team room. We did our homework and found seminars and online training opportunities to build our knowledge base and find other subject matter experts.

In fact, while attending the Mobile Home Boot Camp (who knew there was one?) in San Jose, Texas, we met a former Special Operator and industry giant who became our mentor. I'll call him Steve. He introduced us to other relevant players in the network. Travis and I used the same process we'd used in the military to learn about complex problems and build strong teams.

By connecting with a handful of mentors who helped us reduce our learning curve and avoid the lethal pitfalls of real estate, we turned one singlewide trailer in North Carolina into a multimillion-dollar portfolio in about eight years. There is absolutely no way we could ever have done that on our own. And even if there were, it would have taken much longer.

Fill your team room with mentors who want to make an impact with you and who can keep you from making catastrophic mistakes.

It was the tribe we-built around this collaborative discipline that allowed us to build a large real estate portfolio, secure favorable long-term loans, and build systems that made us industry leaders and, ultimately, financially free. You can do the exact same thing in whatever discipline you choose — whether it's working for someone else or starting your own business.

Keeping the light on in your team room keeps you in touch with teammates who can ease transition woes by sharing the miles they've already run; it gives you a new tribe of relevant players; it keeps you from making fatal errors by connecting you with impactful mentors; and it gives us the strength of others to leverage into playing a much bigger game.

Mission America tip: As you get clearer on your purpose in life after the military, start researching these areas:

Who are peers from your organization who have transitioned well and are reaching back out?

What are the most relevant lessons learned for:

Accessing your GI Bill or transferring it to your kids?

Learning all of your options on the VA Loan?

Readjusting your separation/retirement pay and life insurance/SGLI to meet the new realities of civilian life?

Maximizing your health screening if transitioning before separation from service or...

Maximizing your retirement physical to ensure you get your VA benefits?

Who are industry or discipline leaders in the career arena you're interested in?

What self-study can you pursue? (There is so much available online.)

What service-based nonprofit groups are out there that can help you build your team room?

Are there mentors in your local area or online? (American Dream U is a great place to start.)

Does the Small Business Administration have national or local programs that you can reach into?

Throughout this book, you've seen a common theme that you already have so many tools inside of you for use in transition to the civilian world. Now, with a tribe of folks in our corner and a powerful story, we need to tap into our appreciation for military intelligence and build a picture of what we're up against and the opportunities that lie within that intelligence picture.

18

A NEW USE FOR 'INTEL'

"How bad is it?" I asked. I closed my eyes and waited for the answer.

"Pretty bad."

Cold needles in my skin — I opened my eyes as I stood in our bedroom beside my wife Monty. She looked at me straight in the eyes. "Pretty bad," she said again. "We don't even really have enough for Christmas presents for the kids."

"Dammit," I said louder than I meant to. I didn't want our three little boys to hear us. My blood was boiling. I was angry, not at my wife, but at myself for how upset I was getting — for the mess we were in.

My wife was also upset. But she was generally calmer than me in these situations. I had been through all kinds of crazy stress as a Green Beret — had worked in shitty places all over the world — but for some reason money issues stressed me out bad.

And this moment was as bad as anything I could remember.

We had barely enough in our checking account to pay our monthly bills. Our savings account was a big goose egg and had been as dry as sand for years. Our credit cards were maxed out on ridiculously high interest rates.

Our mounting debt was through the roof and several bills were overdue. I had no investments. Well, I suppose you could count a meager little Thrift Savings Plan (TSP) account that I couldn't even access without the penalties taking it down to zero.

We didn't even own our own home. We were renting.

Now, with Christmas right around the corner, how would we buy presents for our three little boys? I felt like a complete failure.

"How could this happen?!" I groaned. "How could we be in such a mess?" Here I was a major in the U.S. Army Special Forces and my whole financial picture was a disaster.

Angry. Scared. Ashamed.

I swore to myself, "NEVER AGAIN." That was December 11th, 2007. I meant every word.

THE LIFETIME REWARD OF BUILDING INTELLIGENCE

Monty and I turned things around over the next few years. We became cash-flow positive. And despite numerous frustrations along the way, we became financially free by the time I retired from the military about five years later.

Since then, I've learned I wasn't alone in these types of money problems.

CHOOSING THE TOOLS FOR YOUR JOURNEY

"What am I going to do now?" Ever ask this question? The return to civilian professional life after a life in the military is fraught with financial and professional challenges. This is where the questions build up like floodwaters against a dam.

What will your new profession be? Will you enter the private sector as an employee? Should you start a business? Should you go to school on your G.I. Bill? Is it better to stay close to the life you know by pursuing work as a government contractor or DOD employee? Or is it time to put that gun away and write that book you've always wanted to write? Perhaps you can continue your higher purpose by starting a nonprofit corporation?

Maybe it's a combination of several of these. For me it was.

These are big decisions.

Regardless of what you select, how you prepare for this decision is a tool you already have as a warrior. Intelligence is key.

BUILD YOUR MISSION AMERICA INTELLIGENCE PICTURE

Think about every mission you executed in the military. It didn't matter whether it was tactical training in the U.S., a six-month Navy 'Float' in the Indian Ocean, or an air patrol over Bosnia; preparation was a key component of every one of these missions. And at the heart of this preparation was intelligence preparation of the environment — or *IPB*, as many of us called it.

Can you imagine executing any of these military missions without significant military intelligence on the front end? Of course not? Then, why do it any differently in a mission as big as transition?

Intelligence preparation of the environment is part of our mission planning process. It's how you think about the enemy (or in this case, struggles) we'll face, the terrain, weather…everything that could adversely or positively affect your mission. Your transition should be no different. For Mission America, it's *transition intelligence preparation of the environment*.

There are several types of transition intelligence:

1. FINANCIAL INTELLIGENCE

Understanding some basic financial parameters can make all the difference in this new life of yours.

Here's the deal. Most of us just don't have the basic financial knowledge we need to thrive in civil society. I didn't.

This is a major gap among many warriors and their families. Don't beat yourself up on this one. Most civilian folks don't have it either. This type of financial intelligence is not something we were taught in school.

The U.S. military sure as hell didn't provide any financial intelligence training, did it? In fact, most of your financial issues were dumbed down by Uncle Sam and handled by the military support system. The military created this security blanket so you could remain mission focused. But that's not your world anymore, is it?

Now, as you look at transition, there are distinct knowledge gaps in your basic understanding of personal and professional financial issues.

I was clueless when it came to financial intelligence. For me, the book *Rich Dad, Poor Dad* by

Robert Kiyosaki made a big difference in my financial intelligence, and more importantly, how I thought about wealth in relation to my life's goals.

The author, Robert Kiyosaki, is a former Marine gunship pilot who has had his ups and downs in life, but I like his view on cash flow. While this book doesn't necessarily show you a step-by-step plan on how to do it, it gives you insights on how to think differently about wealth, and building assets that work for you in the form of passive income (more on that in just a second).

Another great book to increase your financial intelligence is *Millionaire Master Plan* by Roger James Hamilton. Where Kiyosaki emphasizes entrepreneurialism and investing as the only way to freedom, Roger Hamilton presents a range of options to meeting your financial goals, including being an employee for someone else.

I encourage you to learn about different types of income (active, portfolio, and passive), assets, liabilities, and cash flow. I also hope that you'll consider these basic financial components in the context of *financial freedom*.

Financial freedom is when your passive income from assets is greater than your expenses.

Financial freedom will make it much easier to redirect and pursue your passion. You don't have to be financially free to be happy, but it sure helps. Even if you choose not to pursue it, just knowing what it is can make all the difference in the path you choose for yourself. Now let's look at the intelligence applications to help you find or prepare for your next profession.

2. TECHNICAL INTELLIGENCE

The next type of intelligence I recommend is technical intelligence. This is intelligence related to the type of profession or discipline you intend to pursue in your post-military life. This often involves homework and self-study. The earlier, the better.

The more research you do beforehand, the better off you'll be in transition. Even if you don't know your passion yet, don't sweat it. Warriors are good at intel work and that's just what this is. In the absence of clarity, apply rigor and discipline to your IPB process.

Consider this process akin to the area study and route planning you would do before a big deployment or combat mission. This means deep diving into the endeavors that align with your new dreams and goals.

"Man, I think this training is more intensive than the combat deployments." This is what a Green Beret weapons sergeant said to me in 2004. We were going through a rigorous six-month pre-mission training event in anticipation of Afghanistan. He echoed what most of us were feeling.

Notice I said six months for pre-mission training. Most of us have spent at least that amount of time preparing for a big deployment. During that time, every fiber of our being is singularly focused on one thing — the deployment. Why would we treat intel prep for transition any differently?

Building technical intelligence is a crucial step in turning your dreams into a post-transition reality. Let's look at a real-world example.

INTELLIGENCE AND TRAILERS (A CASE STUDY)

For me, building my technical intelligence involved learning about real estate, affordable housing, and property management.

Was I crazy passionate about affordable housing real estate? No, I wasn't. But it gave me passive income and a platform to chase other passions that 'lit me up.'

Once I decided to pursue this real estate niche as a part of my transition plan, I had to identify my knowledge gaps and then build out my knowledge through online courses, self-study, and seminars. When needed, I shelled out money and invested in my technical education.

This technical capacity building was an inherent part of my transition preparation. I followed the same approach of building technical intelligence as I became a writer, speaker, and even for starting nonprofits like the one that produced this book.

3. SOCIAL INTELLIGENCE FOR MENTORS AND NETWORKS

I also sought out mentors and peers in my new real estate network to help me overcome the gaps I couldn't bridge on my own. But it was the process of intel preparation that led me to do that. Intel preparation was how I found my new network.

Whether you are improving your financial intelligence, your technical intelligence, or both, it's important to build a network around this effort. Warriors are good at this anyway.

You understand the value in reaching across organizational seams and into unknown areas to find experts on complex problems.

Ask yourself, "Who is crushing it and succeeding in the field I want to go into?" Then put a plan together of how you'll connect with them. Then start reaching out to them. Don't limit yourself here.

It doesn't matter if you know them or not. Map out a way to connect to study them, learn from their best practices, even connect with them personally. I have done this with *New York Times* best-selling author Steven Pressfield, world-renowned public speaker Bo Eason, and Wharton negotiating Professor Stuart Diamond, just to name a few.

You have to do this if you are going to succeed in many of the military battle zones we work in. This is no different. You need to build new networks around your new transition challenges.

Here is a common mistake that many warriors make: They don't stretch their comfort zones on networks. This is an epic mistake. You need to build new networks in addition to your old networks. I need you to do this. Will you?

MY BATTALION COMMANDER NEVER PICKED A DECENT STOCK FOR ME

Would you get medical advice for your kids from your squad leader? Of course not. So why would you rely on your chain of command for transition perspective on skills outside the military?

Your chain of command plays an essential role in transitioning out of the service. But what about after?

Over-relying on the folks you know in the military, without any outside input, is ill-advised for transition. It's usually not a good idea to ask your team sergeant about financial intelligence (unless he's financially free) or your platoon sergeant on how to design a business plan (unless she's kicking ass with her own small business).

I would refrain from asking your battalion Air NCO how to start a nonprofit. And even your battalion command sergeant major — as seasoned as that old fart may be — is probably not the right guy to tell you how to conduct an interview that endears you to potential employers.

Of course, there are exceptions, but in most cases you need to seek out new experts — beyond your military security blanket.

When I look back on my path to financial and personal freedom, I think about several things that made a big difference in my success. Probably the most impactful, however, was finding coaches.

COACHES AND MENTORS

Some people refer to them as mentors. It doesn't matter what you call them. Get one. Get several.

Ever see an Olympic athlete without a coach? Why would you be any different?

Find people who have successfully walked the ground you would like to walk.

Some may be veterans. Some may not. Many of my coaches never served in the military, but that's good! They have run miles in other key areas that I care about.

And they want to help me discover new best practices that reduce my learning curves, which would have been much more difficult on my own. (For real estate, the lessons I might have learned on my own could have been catastrophic. I don't know about you, but I'm not taking that chance.)

These types of coaches are people I look up to

much like many of the mentors I had in the military. They embody the level of fulfillment and success I want to achieve in some aspect of my life. Stare at what they are doing like an infant learning to walk who visually drinks in the mechanics of every adult who walks past her.

If you want to start a fishing guide service, then you should seek out coaches that have succeeded in that type of business. In fact, find the very best ones.

Don't limit yourself.

In this age of hyper-connectivity, it's easier than you think to find quality coaches. But it does take some effort.

GIVE AND TAKE

And it's not about just milking someone for information and experience either. It's a relationship that has 'give and take' woven throughout. For example, I am learning social media from an Internet marketing guru named Kris who wants to help veterans, but I am also helping him connect his noble 'Operation Camo Cookies' to the distribution nodes that can push these goodies out to our warriors.

Give and take, baby. Reciprocity is a beautiful thing. You should have learned this as a warrior or military spouse. Build it out and use it.

Coaches can help you build your intelligence to fill your knowledge gaps, prepare your plan, and pursue your action steps. They know when to let you make mistakes and when to intervene and prevent game-ending blunders.

Pros need coaches. Find coaches for all pillars in your life. Personally and professionally, coaches can shorten the distance across those vast transition gaps and accelerate our path to happiness. Some coaches may cost money. Big deal — if it gets you there faster and with more of yourself intact, I say do it.

Most of the hyper-successful people I emulate in the private sector have coaches. Beware of bad coaching, though. In the long run, it's a heck of a lot more expensive to work with an amateur coach on the cheap, than it is to hire a pro.

RUCK UP AND MOVE OUT

No matter how much preparation we do, and how many quality mentors we have...there is no substitute for action, even in the absence of clarity.

Don't overthink it. It won't ever be perfect. At first, a 70 percent knowledge base may be all you can obtain of the financial or professional intel picture you want. No worries. Then it's time for action. As my team sergeant used to say, "Sir, we have all the info we're going to get just sitting here. We gotta ruck up and figure the rest out as we go." That's so true in transition.

Good intel work is key, but so is momentum. As you start to "ruck up" and step into this new world, many things will start to come together and become more clear.

Your financial and technical intelligence should be informed by your redirection of purpose. This will give you the clarity you need for your next professional endeavor: school, entrepreneur, author, employee, or nonprofit organization.

Goal-directed action is the key here.

Your warrior ethos, if you allow it, will power your professional and personal engines in this new mission.

Now let's go to Part III, the final portion of our time together, and see what it really means to come home.

Part III

Return —
What Right Looks Like

19

COMING HOME: IT TAKES A VILLAGE...AND A WARRIOR

BROOKLYN, NEW YORK, 2014

"Returning home from war isn't new," said Shawn Coyne. Shawn is partners with best-selling author Steven Pressfield in the Black Irish Publishing Company. Shawn never served, but you should still listen to him.

He's done a lot of work in supporting veteran transition. His company published the excellent military transition book by former Marine Dave Danello, aptly named *The Return*.

I was interviewing Shawn and Dave on the challenges and opportunities of veteran transition. "Ever since the days of Odysseus, soldiers have struggled to return home."

Think about it. As warriors, we have each been on our own *Hero's Journey,* haven't we?

DEFINING THE RETURN HOME

Like Homer's mythical hero, we return home as changed individuals, trying to figure out where we fit in. That's not a bad thing.

In fact, it's perfectly normal. It's a timeless undertaking.

What does it mean to return? There are so many definitions out there, but I think we need to look at it from the perspective of the warrior *and* the citizen:

For veterans: RETURN means reintegrating into your communities both personally and professionally, so that you are able to pursue your redirected purpose and have your shot at a life of happiness and prosperity.

There are no guarantees here. No promises or entitlements, except an honest and authentic run at achieving the very things guaranteed by our Constitution that you and your loved ones put on hold while preserving this right through military service for your fellow Americans.

For citizens: RETURN means the reintegration of warriors who are high performers and complex problem solvers. It means bringing home our husbands, wives, sons, daughters, brothers, sisters, dads, moms, and neighbors. More importantly it means bringing home leaders who are hardwired to lead our communities, our nation, and our children to a better future.

RETURN also means there is a small percentage of warriors who, because of the grievous effects of combat injuries, will rely on citizen and government support for the rest of their lives.

As I point out in Chapter 8, this "damaged goods" narrative has unfortunately become the central story for veteran transition. While we should look at veterans in a more participatory light, Americans should never forget this reality of a small group of wounded warriors who need our perpetual care as well.

IT'S DIFFERENT FOR EACH OF US

Even with a consistent definition, returning home looks different for everybody these days. Some of you will stay around military bases for the Veterans Administration medical benefits (trying to keep a straight face on that one) or move to hubs where follow-on government employment or contracting offer opportunities.

Others will go home to the places you are originally from, where there are no military bases or support networks. The same is true for many National Guard and Reserve veterans who transition back home after years of active service in this long war and settle back home into towns where there is almost no military presence.

And still some of you will go to brand-new places. Maybe that exotic place abroad, like a sleepy mountain town in the Republic of Panama where you conducted missions long ago (or is that just me?).

Or maybe you're going to a new town in the U.S. that offers unique opportunities to start fresh.

Here is the good news. No matter where you go, there is a huge support base of American citizens, in communities across the country, who are committed to helping you return home and find your path. But this is not an entitlement for you — just like your military-based ethos, this community support is a precious resource.

This needs to be done right, which means changing the narrative and how we tell our story, as discussed in Chapter 8.

HELPING CIVILIANS UNDERSTAND US

Returning home involves veterans understanding the mindset of many civilian employers and community members.

Remember, while we've been immersed in a military culture and surrounded by warriors, a very small percentage of America serves in the military. Understanding the military is not as intuitive as we might think.

"We don't always get you guys. Truth be told, we're a little bit intimidated by you — we just see you as badasses and we're a little uncomfortable around you." These were cautions from Tampa attorney Kendall Almerico as he explained how many business owners in his circle feel around veterans.

If this is a consistent narrative in some circles, then we are not communicating effectively with our fellow Americans as we come home. I hear this not just from employers, but from veterans themselves.

"Employers don't know who the hell we are, or what we do," retired Army Master Sergeant Dan Hilty said to me as we discussed challenges in veterans finding jobs in today's tight job market.

We can overcome this.

IT STARTS WITH US

There will be challenges. There will be ups and downs. It will take time. Rather than just disappearing off the grid claiming "The civilian world sucks and no one gets us," I suggest you go the other way.

Make deeper connections with our fellow citizens.

Enough with the entitlement narrative. Enough with "No one understands us." Regardless of sacrifice, it doesn't suit warriors at all. This is not just the responsibility of our civilian population but also of the veteran.

All of us have to manage our expectations, as well as those of our loved ones, that transition back into society is a process, not an overnight event. It's not easy, but we have to be patient with our progress and tolerant of a community that doesn't quite understand the miles we've run.

Returning home in transition is a combined effort between the civilian and the warrior. This will define the lasting strength of our nation. (This essential human connection is why we formed MISSION AMERICA as a nonprofit.)

For reconnecting warriors and civilians, let's start by looking at how NOT to do it, and how we can honor and restore some healing to a very special segment of our veteran community in the process.

20

FROM DOG CRAP TO YELLOW RIBBONS

ASHEVILLE, NORTH CAROLINA, 2002

"They threw dog shit on me." I had never seen him like this. He usually had a very present demeanor, but now he was a thousand miles away as he sat right beside me. His voice softened. My uncle Jerry, usually a tough guy, talked about his redeployment from Vietnam.

"I remember coming back. It felt good to finally be coming home. I had my dress white uniform on and these protesters were calling me 'baby killer' and all kinds of vile stuff. Then they threw dog shit all over my white uniform — all over me."

Profound sadness caused his voice to shake just a little as he said, "You just don't forget that."

His voice trailed off as, once more, he suppressed the years of pain, and settled back into the real world as we watched television. Fox News was covering modern-day warriors returning from

Afghanistan being met by cheering crowds waving flags and playing patriotic music shortly after 9-11-2001. That memory stuck with me.

This can never happen again.

WARRIORS ADRIFT — AN AMERICAN TRAGEDY

Citizens of America, warriors must be allowed to come home. Failure to reintegrate into civil society can be devastating for veterans.

Many of our brothers and sisters from the Vietnam War did not receive the embrace from their homeland that they should have. Just like my Uncle Jerry, many were treated horribly by protestors.

Just as painful, many others who had simply done what their country had asked them to do as young men, in the boiling cauldron of combat, were ignored when they came back home. Or worse, they were made to feel as if they had committed some form of atrocity.

The impact of this treatment by their own citizenry, after enduring the horrors of war, is indescribable, and has a lot to do with many of the PTSD and other systemic issues within the Vietnam veteran community.

Many still suffer from this horrible treatment today.

Society denied these heroes that essential rite of passage usually afforded to every warrior who returns home from war — the embrace of the people he fought for.

This was a low point in American history and should never be repeated.

While much of this book focuses on helping today's post–9-11 veterans, we should place greater emphasis on healing the wounds and bringing home our Vietnam and Korean War veterans as well. It is never too late.

I'll start.

To those brave Vietnam War heroes, I say "Thank you for your sacrifice. And <u>WELCOME HOME!</u> Please forgive us for not saying it sooner. We need you and your leadership more than ever."

Mission America tip: Civilians come up and thank me all the time for my service. This means a lot. But if you want to have an even deeper and more healing impact on our nation, whenever you meet a Vietnam or Korean War veteran from these often-forgotten wars, look them in the eyes, and say something like this: "*Welcome home. [Pause.] I am sorry we didn't say it to you sooner, and we are so grateful for all you've done for our country.*" Then enjoy the depth of connection that is impossible to describe in this book.

Teach your kids to do this as well. These warriors are not hard to spot. Many Vietnam veterans will wear hats and T-shirts proudly proclaiming their service — start there.

Also, if these veterans have their wives with them, thank them as well. My aunt Geraldine speaks with the same profound sadness as her husband Jerry about how horribly she and other military family members were treated during this period.

They sacrificed a lot and it's never too late to say "thank you."

Things are much better today than they were back then, but there is still a lot of work to be done.

21

A WORD TO CITIZENS...

WASHINGTON, D.C., 2016

"I never served. But that's the reason why I am standing in front of you guys today." Phil always says something like this when he's standing on the stage talking to service members. His 'aw shucks' demeanor hides how impressive he is as a real estate entrepreneur and businessman.

Civilians, don't let your comfort zone hold you back. Phil Randazzo, founder of American Dream U, is an example of how to serve even if you weren't in the military. Phil saw a gap in how veterans are prepared for transition by the Department of Defense. To fill this gap, often on his own dime, he connects active duty members with kick-ass entrepreneurs in a no-nonsense training workshop known as VETRACON.

American Dream U demonstrates just how critical civilians are in every aspect of veteran transition. If you are a civilian who never served, but wants to make a difference in how our veterans RETURN, this chapter is written just for you.

THE CRITICAL ROLE OF THE CIVILIAN SPONSOR

Without you, as we saw in the last chapter on Vietnam transition, veterans are lost. We simply can't come home without a caring community to welcome us back home. Here are a few thoughts for Mission America for our civilian teammates to consider.

Veterans greatly appreciate the outpouring of gratitude. Those airport greetings and heartfelt words of praise when you come up to us in public mean more than I can describe in these pages. But everywhere I go, folks like you are asking how you can do more. Here we go:

Don't wait for someone to tell you how to do it. Just start. Take a page from Phil and be the catalyst that reconnects warriors and their families to your community. Imagine this:

There is a small canyon. The canyon is big enough that it is impossible to jump over.

On the near side of the canyon where you are standing, there is your wonderful community filled with cool people and local opportunity. But like most places in America, it is struggling. Solid leaders and problem solvers are sorely needed.

On the other side of the small canyon stands an amazing little group of men, women, and families who are trying to figure out a way across the canyon. They are unusually talented leaders and experienced problem solvers. But there is just one problem.

They are struggling to find their way across that

canyon.

In your possession, on the community side of the canyon, is a portable metal footbridge that you can simply push across and allow them to cross over.

It's no big deal to you, but putting that bridge in place makes all the difference to those veterans on the other side.

In other words, they can't get across without you. This is exactly how you should be thinking about veteran transition.

Sure, that canyon of transition can be a little daunting, but when civilians kick that footbridge over, the gap becomes insignificant. Isn't this how we should all be looking at the problem?

There are plenty of government and large, nonprofit transition programs out there. But the most impactful veteran outreach and transition programs are at the community level.

The bigger programs are great. But local efforts have a much more pronounced effect on our veterans, and our community.

All big issues really are local issues.

EVERY COMMUNITY NEEDS WHAT YOU GOT

Do research about veteran transition programs or VA programs in your area. Talk to local veterans in your community and find out what the gaps are. This is where you can assist and play a big role. There are so many ways you can use your civilian expertise to help out once you identify the pain points. Here is one example:

Gary Marriage Jr. is a financial advisor who works in Crystal River, Florida. He works with older veterans to ensure they receive the Medicaid and Social Security benefits they are entitled to, but don't realize they are eligible for.

Gary has helped hundreds of veterans claim tens of thousands of dollars in benefits they were completely unaware of. He learned about these programs when training as a financial advisor.

He does the work on a volunteer basis, in the small places in between, even when no one else is looking. "I just like seeing the promise fulfilled to all of our heroes who gave so much to my family and me," Gary humbly told me. This is just one example of civilian folks stepping in to assist.

Take a look inside you. I guarantee there are some unique skills that could be of immense support to our veterans in transition. Still not sure what you can do? Try this one on for size:

STEPPING UP WHEN NO ONE IS LOOKING

Justin is a counselor at Tampa General Hospital and he helps folks with spinal cord injuries reintegrate into the world. But there is more.

Justin is a paraplegic himself. Although he's paralyzed from the waist down, Justin is an extreme athlete. He competes on Tampa General's adaptive Rugby Team. Affectionately (and appropriately, I might add) known as "murderball," this high-performance sport lets spinal cord injury patients play full out and compete in an exciting and invigorating arena.

But that's not the best part. Half the team are civilians with spinal cord injuries, but the other half are veterans. The civilians on this team embody the Mission America narrative of connecting warriors and citizens at a community level.

Justin and his civilian buddies started coaxing veterans onto their team years ago. Many of these warriors had crawled inside a shell. "I was in a bad place," the Special Ops NCO Sua told me. "When I was shot by the Taliban years ago, my injuries had changed my whole life. I was really depressed. This connection to the Generals has changed my life."

This is the lesson that must be captured and amplified. Civilian leaders with debilitating injuries found a way to leverage their challenge into a connection point with local veterans. How about you? How can you connect?

Most veterans don't need a handout, but would love a hand up. Sharing your experience on how to build a résumé, mentoring on how to write a business plan, or just providing connections to other potential employers or resources in your networks can be such a big deal.

TRY THIS

Welcoming a military family to the neighborhood can have a huge impact. Transition is a pretty scary monster for most veterans. This is a world very familiar to you, but civilian life seems like Mars to a veteran. Your civilian perspective on so many various aspects of personal and professional life is more helpful than you will ever know.

Take the time. Have a conversation. Listen deeply to a veteran in transition, and you'll see multiple places you can connect. I guarantee it.

WHAT NOT TO DO

One more thing, and I almost hate to bring it up, because it's so obvious as something <u>not to do</u>. But

I have to because it still happens.

No matter how close your relationship is to a veteran, don't ask him if he killed anyone. Or even, "So what's it like over there?" Combat is a corrosive environment that sticks with a warrior in different ways.

Pass this on to your kids as well. Often, they just innocently want to know what it's like. But it can take a veteran backward in some very debilitating ways.

The closer we connect to you, the better transition will go.

Unless you are specifically trained in this kind of work, casually talking about killing or traumatic violence is not a healthy endeavor for any veteran or community member.

Additionally, this can trigger some rough emotions for a veteran — not all, but some. To talk about combat can be very difficult and take a lot of time.

It was over a year before I could publicly say the names of some of my dearest friends who were killed. I am still working through some of the rough patches. But I learned to do it through the healing power of story. The same is possible for you. That's just how it goes.

Our veterans will talk when the time is right, but for now, they are still processing all of it. Be patient with us and we'll move through this together. Instead, let's focus on the important task of the future and moving forward in our communities.

22

CONCLUSION

Transition and life after the military is a crazy ride.

You're not alone. I experienced it, and many other veterans I work with experienced it also.

Believe it or not, many of these things are actually good problems to have.

A life of prosperity and happiness is not as far away as you think. But it can seem far away. Especially after you've spent the first part of your adult life doing work that was so naturally congruent with your warrior ethos.

Just know this: Much of what you'll need to transition and lead in the civilian world, you already have.

You've done enough hard training events, and dangerous, complex missions to trust the process even when things are not very clear.

Military service has given us the physical and mental discipline to start each day with energy and focus — to see the challenges before

us, and the opportunities that lie just beyond the horizon, even when others can't. It's just who we are.

Focus that discipline on finding your own purposeful path and the passion(s) to feed it, as if you were preparing for another mission.

Breathe into this new reality, and embrace this phase of your life. You've put your dreams on hold all this time so that others could live their dreams. Now it's your turn. It's your mission…Mission America.

Good luck, and I'll see you on the high ground.

De Oppresso Liber,
Scott Mann

ABOUT THE AUTHOR

LTC (Retired) Scott Mann is a Special Forces officer who retired in November 2012. Scott spent almost 23 years in the Army, and about 18 years in Special Forces and Special Operations. Scott spent 10 years in 7th Special Forces Group (Airborne) deploying to Central and South America, Iraq, and Afghanistan. Scott is a real estate entrepreneur, public speaker, best-selling author, military analyst, and advocate for veterans and veterans' families. He lives in Tampa, Florida with his wife Monty and his boys: Cody, Cooper, and Brayden.

Scott's email is: scott@theheroesjourney.org

How you can help: It's up to us. We need your help to bring our warriors and families home. Go to www.theheroesjourney.org, donate, and become part of the mission.

This is our time — this is our mission — this is MISSION AMERICA!

SCOTT MANN SPEAKING TOPICS

Mission America Founder, LTC (Retired) Scott Mann is an experienced and motivational storyteller. His speeches will help warriors prepare for transition and help civilians find better ways to bring our warriors home. Below are some of Scott's most popular military transition speeches.

Mission America Keynote
Scott has given this speech to service members and their families on military bases across America. The powerful message in this talk is that warriors already have most of the tools they need from their life in the military to fuel a successful transition. It's all about re-directing to a new mission...MISSION AMERICA.

Your Story - The Ultimate Warrior Transition Asset This
speech has become the most watched video on the American Dream U website. In this inspirational talk, Scott will help warriors and their families get beyond the transactional resume and help them tap into the most powerful asset they have...their story.

Bridging the Gap
Understanding military members and the obstacles they face isn't easy. This powerful talk is designed for civilians, business leaders, employers, and other patriots who are looking for ways to re-connect to transitioning warriors and their families. Scott will share inside perspective

on the challenges service members face in transition. And more importantly, Scott will show how civilian leaders can directly influence the ability of these high performing warriors and families to transition home, and bring their dynamic skill and capability back to our businesses and communities.

To book Scott as a speaker, contact us at   contact@theheroesjourney.org

Made in the USA
Middletown, DE
25 October 2022